The Heron in Isfahan

Recollections of a girl on the hippie trail

by Caroline Born

www.carolineborn.co.uk

Published by

heart song press

Prepared for printing by Hafiz Ladell
for Magic Pocket Productions
Pre-press attention by Jamie Waring of PH Media, Roche, Cornwall
Printed and bound by TJ International Ltd, Padstow, Cornwall

A CIP catalogue record for this book is available from the British Library

ISBN 978-1-9161780-0-7

All artwork and photography by Caroline Born,
except for the photograph of the author in the Turkish
mountains which was taken by John Sefton.

Cover design by Wyn Rainbow

To Izzy,

my fellow traveller

A bright star who fell to earth

in September 2015

Contents

Letts Diary | 1973

Preface

The journey I took was inevitable. I had to open my heart and mind, so I left home and went travelling. Under my belt was the blood of my nature-loving father and my mother's writerly sensibility, but most of me lay dormant. I was hungry to immerse myself in disparate cultures and lifestyles, and the offbeat and colourful were calling. It felt crucial to branch out a long way from the familiar. With my best friend Izzy, I took off across Europe on one-way tickets to Athens. We hadn't planned to stop in Greece for long but when we landed on the hippie trail all plans became possibilities, open to change. When we headed east, war diverted us onto another path.

My little red Collins diary has been sitting in my attic for over forty years. Finding it has opened a window into myself at nineteen and the world in 1973. It measures just four inches by three. As I read the tiny script with my 64-year-old bespectacled eyes, my younger self turns to look at me. Her face says life is free and exciting. She carries little baggage, her mind and rucksack are light. I look back in surprise and envy at the magical protection of her naiveté. The diary has returned her to me. In meeting her, will I discover what has changed in me, and what has not?

The smallness of the pages I countered with my rapidograph, an architect's pen with the tiniest of nibs I'd used for my A level art. I wrote down everything I did and all I felt. The little diary was my pitstop and my handhold. The memories are clear of all the events that chased each other like swallows, because my eyes were wide open all year. My diary tells of the details: the ingredients of a meal eaten at the top of a gorge in Crete, the pictures pasting the walls of a fisherman's hut in Israel, and exactly how the heron stood in the river near Isfahan. The narrative of my intense feelings was minutely recorded, safely encapsulated I'd thought, always to be private. Page after page reveals my unconscious innocent assumption that I knew all about life.

I feel greater by meeting her. Absorbing her, I have more of myself. She set the course of my adult life when she flew like an arrow away from home. She knew we would meet again, as in Israel she wrote to me:

> *If you are reading now and you look in the mirror, maybe you could see the old eyes of her through the changes.*

I'm grateful for her diligence, the still-schoolgirl self who wrote every day in her little diary as she travelled the warm roads of Greece and the Middle East. Her laid-back hippie abandon hadn't discarded her careful prose, still unconsciously ingrained with pleasing teacher.

Devon, August 1973

A few days before I left I was making a blue paisley passport holder to hang around my neck under my clothes. I looked up and out of the window. Making the tiny stitches had quietened me into a reverie and it felt as if the physical preparation was also an inner one. I stared at the perfect blue line of infinity where sea met sky. The waves swished lazily over the sand on the beach below. All was as it ever was. I was in my parents' beautiful home by the sea, yet miles away, moving towards the disappearing line of blue into blue. The arms of the granite house gently enclosed me as I stood staring out and out, but the expanse I felt was inside my body. I felt flooded with relief, knowing something had begun.

Caroline Born
South Milton, Devon. 2019

salcombe
AMSTERDAM
NIS

N
Caspian Sea
Erzurum
Tehran
Istanbul
Isfahan
Mersin
Cyprus
Jerusalem

1

Leaving England

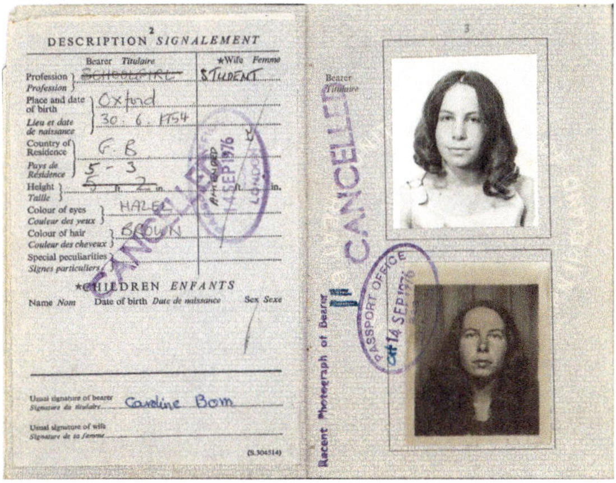

August 30

I'm watching Izzy throw her clothes, one by one, out of the train window. I'm sitting facing her in our compartment and the sliding window is open as wide as it can go. Wrinkling up her nose she holds out another buttoned-up-to-the-neck white blouse and thrusts it out of the window where it flutters wildly and disappears. These crisply ironed blouses were packed firmly in her rucksack before we left with the instruction: 'You must wear something decent in Athens, Isabel.'

White flags flapping maniacally in the wind, then gone.

We were slim, brown, nineteen and beautiful, streaming through the English countryside en route to Athens. We were free. Delightedly and wonderfully free. Free of school, free of parents, and heading for more freedom. Izzy and I shared a love of hippie culture that wove through our clothes, our music, our way of living and even our language. We wore long Indian cotton skirts, thin shirts and sandals. Izzy wore an assortment of silver bangles and rings that jingled night and day.

I carried my small guitar, and together we sang the surreal and haunting tunes of The Incredible String Band to bemused passengers. My modest army surplus rucksack contained my faithful duck-down blue sleeping bag that rolled up to nothing, one pair of brown cotton bell-bottoms, a thin jacket, another shirt and some underwear. I brought my rapidograph pen, a sketchbook, my diary, and a book by Carlos Castaneda. Last but not least was my little sewing kit: a tin soap box covered with intricate brown and crimson leather marquetry I'd found at the back of a drawer at home.

Just before we left I bought four packets of sun-dried bananas. They lasted us four days. I don't remember feeling hungry. Food was the last thing on our minds. It was simply irrelevant.

My diary reads:

Gave up smoking. Woke at 6.30. Izzy's parents drove us to Bruton station. Caught train to Victoria. Managed to renew YHA card first. Left England at 11.00am. Caught the boat to Ostend few hours later. Very unreal situation. Travelled through Belgium and Germany. Minor hassles with a little dark German in the night. Izzy was freaked out. He kept hanging around in the corridor but it was ok. Woken up at 6.30am by two girls we had met from the next door cabin. Half asleep we fell out of the train. Munich station smooth and expensive. Ridiculous prices. Coffee 7 shillings a cup. We went without. Caught train to Athens 8.00. Went across Austrian Alps. Passed the Matterhorn. Met Johnny and Greek guy. Bought us cups of coffee & orange, biscuits etc. Wouldn't accept any thanks. Austria much more beautiful than Yugoslavia. Our cabin invaded by some Yugos at midnight. Very friendly. But it got very claustrophobic. Next day contd. through Yugo. Began to look more like Greece.

2

The Hippie Trail

September 2

> *Woke up to find ourselves in Athens feeling shattered. Set off across the city to find Melina's house under the Acropolis. She was at home and it was an incredible place, a big beautiful house. At first we couldn't suss her. She laughed too much, but she said we could stay.*

Izzy had been given Melina's address by a family friend. I doubt we told her the day we expected to arrive, we simply turned up. We had no idea it would be such a grand house only yards from the Acropolis. The opulence and comfort was a world apart from the basic rest house we'd stayed in the night before. A girl had led us and a group of students from the train wearily across the city, and we had collapsed exhausted on bunk beds. These rags and riches experiences came and went as part of our lives; we didn't remark on them.

Melina was our age, and her parents were out. We stood in a high-ceilinged room surrounded by expensive furniture and she offered us something to eat. We talked, but I was irritated with Izzy. We had been together day and night since we left home, and I needed some time out. I headed up to the Acropolis soothed by the evening cool, drinking in my own space. As I walked, I noticed the local people gently strolling along. The scorch and screech of day gone, all sounds were softened and people were mostly silent or talking quietly. Over the days in Athens I witnessed this evening promenade. People would quietly emerge into the evening air to be calmed by the delicious coolness. Sometimes only the sound of feet drew my attention. Then along the pavements I saw them, freshly dressed and quietly dignified, moving along in twos and family groups as if to honour the evening.

Emerging from the quiet streets I stood facing the Acropolis. The smooth white columns rising to the sky gleamed in the spotlights. I breathed in the peace, my body tiny against the towering columns. Looking at the first column with its flawles curve, its ancient huge perfection stilled me. I turned and leant back, closing my eyes and letting the radiating warmth still held in the stone relax my back. Suddenly an English voice called my name. A school friend was walking towards me. She and her sister had hitched all the way from England. It was surreal to meet her here. We spoke a while, but I disliked the intrusion and wanted to get away. I wanted no reminders of school. My time alone was important, and I left her and walked back.

September 4

Left Melinas for good. Went to "Outside Inn". Things began to improve – they were all really friendly. We slept up on the roof. Met some Americans just returned brown and happy from Kos, a possibility for us.

The cheap and cheerful hippie inn became our base in Athens for the next few days. There were no beds, we didn't think of asking for any and we slept on the roof. I loved it, sleeping high above the city streets, relaxing on hot concrete that never really cooled down during the night. We spent the days wandering around the city, meeting other travellers, hearing travel stories that opened up exciting possibilities of where to go. We were finding our feet in Athens.

The next morning two German women were laughing in the kitchen about one of them nearly having had her bag stolen. A man had squeezed the younger woman's bum and then grabbed her bag. She'd held on to it tightly, then swung it round hard so it hit his head. He had run off.

Although we quickly learnt to ignore unwelcome passes, being hassled by Greek men on the Athens streets was a daily pain. On our first morning walking to Melina's we had been followed by a man who walked next to us, stroking our arms and offering us cigarettes. We ended up shouting at him which finally made him disappear down a side street. Everyone complained of that hot dusty metropolis, but it was the place to get rides, share news of routes or get on a Magic Bus – the hippie-run originators of the tour buses that journeyed huge distances across Europe and the East.

But these drawbacks didn't faze Izzy and me. We had landed on the "Hippie Trail" that ran from Europe to and from Asia, India and Nepal. Athens was a major nexus point along it for those travelling either east or west and, unknowingly, we had arrived during the last years of an incredible freedom of movement. We met brown-faced travellers who had been travelling for years, with stories to tell and songs to sing. We made friendships in minutes. I was excited and happy. I felt I belonged and was accepted simply by being on the road.

The East itself didn't beckon me as much as the meetings with the many clear-eyed travellers inspired with life and the road. I was thrilled and felt I was fluidly merging with a free-floating collection of friendly people like ourselves, living on little, all filled with freedom and choices.

The Outside Inn was where our adventures really

began. Two Americans who also slept on the roof of the inn told us that Syntagma Square was a central meeting place for travellers so we made our way there in the morning. We walked along the hot streets excitedly chatting together through a plethora of smells: retsina, crushed basil and tobacco smoke. Arriving, we saw chairs and tables sprawling out from a café into the square occupied mainly by long-haired travellers sitting and talking. We were welcomed and Izzy recognised a friend from home and went over to him.

A brown-faced woman with long black hair smiled at me and I sat down next to her.

'You've just arrived?'

I stared at her, disconcerted.

'How did you know that?'

She laughed slowly and looked at me and I felt a quietness emanating from her amidst the babble of voices, waiters calling to each other, the rattling of glasses and cups and the traffic nearby.

'Well . . . '

She fingered her long beautiful string of beads, each one a universe of glittering green and orange hues. Then she picked up a soft paper packet and took out a little green cigarette and lit it.

'I guess you look like everyone . . . but I can feel somehow . . . you've not been on the road.'

She smiled at me again, this time a beam from ear to ear. 'Welcome to crazy Athens! I'm Sohani. Have a bidi.' And she offered me one of the little green roll ups. Seeing my blank face she added, 'Indian cigarette?'

I took one and smiled back sheepishly, telling her my name.

I'd been feeling I was one and the same as everyone else, that I already belonged in this tribe and was equal to all. But Sohani called me out on my inexperience. She saw my greenness instantly.

She looked away across the Square as she inhaled, and I stole a look at her face. Her long silver earrings sparkled against her deep tan. There were some lines around her eyes and she held a steady determination in her look and in the angle of her head. She looked worn but not worn out and she emitted a calm clarity. She wore layers of different multi-coloured skirts and a beautiful embroidered top. I was fascinated by her beauty and distinctness. Her bearing conveyed a confidence that assumed nothing, yet was fully open to life. I hadn't met such human authenticity before. She was clearly well travelled and yes, we were completely different, which she had seen in her first glance. Still looking away she said:

'But that doesn't matter. All we know is that we are here now. Nothing else has any reality like this moment. Right?'

I was glad she had moved on to spiritual ideas. I was

expecting the usual, 'Where have you come from?' and so I agreed eagerly, catching on to her thoughts, elated by the idea that my past could be irrelevant. The idea was not new to me but I had never heard anyone speak it out loud with such assurance.

Then she pulled out of her bag a very worn, square book and handed it to me. The cover was dark purple with a white circle surrounded by the repeating words, "Be Here Now". Looking at me with eyes suddenly intense and sparkling, she began to speak fast.

'This man. Ram Dass. He wrote this. I met him in the Ashram and he is American but he was amazing. There was an energy coming from him like the Indian gurus. Maharajji has taken him as his main disciple. We were all drawn to him. Day after day we sat with him. So much truth from him and spoken in an American voice. It was weird but wonderful. I was looking for a teacher when I arrived in India two years ago. I never expected to find an American. He has helped me see. He is helping me see . . . so much.'

I was amazed to see tears falling from Sohani's eyes. I felt embarrassed and looked down at the book cover, pretending to examine it. I had never seen anyone cry so nakedly and naturally. Her openness about how much she was touched by this man Ram Dass was a surprise.

Izzy came over to our table and listened until Sohani got up to leave. Then I realised I was starving, and we ventured down a side street in search of something to eat. In a smoky little café we chose omelettes. They were cheap and familiar, surprisingly comforting in the midst of so much newness. Sitting on creaky stools on either side of a plastic table we touched base with each other. I told Izzy about my meeting with the strong exotic woman.

'That woman, Izzy, her name is Sohani. She showed me a book called "Be Here Now". I can't believe it's called that. I feel like that. I want to be all here and have nothing to do with the past.'

Izzy exclaimed, 'Yes, that's it. It's just like that. We're here – in the now – forever.' And she opened her arms wide, making curving arcs through the space. We laughed, relishing the feeling. Then leaning towards me over the table she went on,

'I met Lawrence – you know, who worked in Uhuru in Oxford. We had a thing for a while. He's heading to India with a friend, they're waiting for a lift. He said you just hang out for a few days and they'll get one. That's how it is.'

We sat in happy silence listening to the hubbub of Greek voices, mainly men around us in the café, then I pulled my little guitar off my back and strummed our favourite String Band tune. We sang "May The Long Time Sun Shine", exhilarating in the joyful words of love and light. We didn't notice the voices had hushed around us until we finished. Suddenly a hearty cheer and clapping burst from the crowd of swarthy men who had turned to listen. A roar of male voices called out: 'More, more singing'. But we stood up and squeezed out, taken aback by the enthusiastic response. As we walked away we heard a lone male voice sing out a strong lilting melody and the clapping shift to a beat to accompany the voice. We had met the Greek love of playing music and singing.

As we walked along the street I mused:

'You know, it's like I've joined a community that has no fixed place. Even the Greeks, some of them, feel connected too – like back there with our singing. It's a moving-around community. Back home with my parents, you know, I actually felt lonely and cut off doing my spiritual thing. I was on my spiritual path like you, but doing it at home reading Castaneda and the Dhammapada made me feel weird. Being here, it's like coming to my true home.'

Izzy nodded. I knew she understood this feeling of connection.

Over the days and weeks on the hippie trail in Greece, it felt natural to have a connection with the east after middle class England. I felt I had "come home" spiritually. I hadn't realised how starved I was for spiritual nourishment, both outwardly in the form of discussion and ideas and inwardly for inner connection and meditation. Every day I met people who felt like kindred souls, and every hour my inner life was being nourished.

One evening, as I walked up to the open door of the

Outside Inn, a thin brown woman was sitting on the steps. She was jingling some coins in her hands, then throwing them down and studying them closely. She looked up briefly as we greeted, then looked down again intent on her strange exercise. I stood for a moment watching her hands cup together to shake the coins again and pour them in a little waterfall onto the step. She wrote something down in a notebook in her lap and gathered them again to repeat the action. Next to her was a big dark blue book. I was about to climb up to my rooftop sleeping abode, but I was curious.

'What are you doing?'

'Come and see.'

She inclined her head for me to sit.

'I'm Joy. I've seen you around. I'm trying to find out if I should go back east so I'm asking the "I Ching". I'm on the third throw.'

'Oh, the "I Ching", yeah sure.'

I didn't want to give away yet again I was a fledgling traveller so I feigned understanding. But I thought it looked like a kind of divination as she threw the coins down again on the stone step and wrote something in her book. I sat down next to her hoping she'd say more, and without looking up, she said:

'I had some yarrow stalks but these Chinese coins feel more right. A friend gave them to me in Goa.'

And she opened her hands to show me three small coins with holes in them inscribed with strange shapes. I took them and turned them over in my hand. Taking them back she went on: 'They are simpler than the stalks. You add them together depending which side they fall.'

She picked up the blue book beside her and held it to her thin chest. 'My constant friend. Heavy but so worth it. I ask it everything. It's led me down some strange roads, and I trust it. You use it?'

'Actually no, in fact actually . . . no I haven't.' I couldn't pretend in the face of her direct question and I waited for her, like Sohani, to comment on my inexperience. But she was too engrossed, more interested in telling me about it.

'It's so important to be clear about your question. Then the I Ching can get where you're at.'

I came clean: 'So, how do you do it? '

She looked at me for a moment, then laughed.

'Ok. You throw the coins and add them up. Tails is two and heads is three. You do that six times and then see on the chart which hexagrams you've thrown. Then you look them up in the book to get the reading. It's synchronicity. You focus on the question and the falling coins pick up on the energy and the answer happens. Jung, Carl Jung brought it to the west some years back, but it's ancient. Used by the Chinese for eons. Some people say, "Be Here Now" is their bible but for me it's the "I Ching". Much wiser.'

I sat with Joy till it was too dark to see as she read her answers aloud from the I Ching, pondering on their meaning. Finally she closed the book and stood up.

'Basically it's telling me it's favourable to cross the great water, so that's what I'll do. There's a lift heading for Afghanistan tomorrow and I'll take it. It's a metaphor of course. There's not much water on that road.'

Laughing, she concluded: 'Just dry old land, but it's telling me it's good to do. I wasn't sure but now I'm clear.'

As I climbed into my sleeping bag and looked up at the stars I wondered at Joy's faith in her old Chinese book and how she let the falling coins divine her path. I thought about her travelling off in the morning carrying the great tome in her rucksack, imagining her on the dusty road heading north up through Greece, Turkey and onwards to Afghanistan, asking it questions as she went.

Izzy and I were beginning to oscillate in an ambiance of spontaneity and chance freed up by the lack of routine and structure. I felt such joy when events and meeting collided in synchrony. Discovering that this ancient book had honed this state as a technique to be used as a means of guidance confirmed my trust in the unexpected. On the road things occurred with the same synchronicity as falling coins. We were in magical territory and we felt as if all the forces were with us.

September 5

Wandered into the park and sewed on the grass. Met three Swiss guys and Richard, Queens College Cambridge... They were catching the ferry to Ios. Back again at the Outside Inn. Decided to sleep outside downstairs in the courtyard. Benjamin wanted us to come to his party in the kitchen but we were totally crashed out. Yet woken up a few hours later by nice smells drifting through the air. Was invited to partake of some very effective hashish. A nice lazy evening in Athens.

Sharing dope was part of the culture. It enabled a loosening of conversation, feelings and ideas and cut through shyness and the awkwardness of language differences. I experienced relaxation, laughter and being at ease with people. Occasionally I would feel euphoric when I was singing or drumming or somewhere especially beautiful. Izzy and I accepted smokes when they were offered, taking in a little to enjoy the camaraderie that came with it.

Life was interwoven with spirituality, and the experience of being in the moment central to it. I found a copy of Ram Dass's book that Sohani had introduced me to at the Outside Inn and started reading it avidly. Sitting in the courtyard head down, I looked up to see a small brown face smiling at me, with flashing blue eyes and a halo of red hair. He nodded at the book.

'Good reading?'

'It's amazing. The guy gave up everything, even being

like, a professor at Harvard.'

'Yeah, he did real surrender, and his book, it's unique. I know the books that come around 'cos I give rides and meet people. I think he's the first Westerner to write about being a yogi. Kind of like a manual. And the title is it really. "Be Here Now". That's the message. Have you read the bit about Maharajji taking acid?'

'No.'

'Well . . .'

My new friend made himself comfortable, sitting cross-legged on the ground next to me.

'I'm Zeb by the way. I'm waiting till I get a full load to head back to Delhi. Had a bit of trouble with the brakes but I'm getting them sorted. All part of the dance with an old bus!'

He laughed as he folded his legs in half lotus on the flagstones and I stared at the sole of his foot facing the sky. It was dark brown, nearly black. His eyes followed mine.

'Yeah, my feet. I drive barefoot – to feel the engine better. They tell me what's going on. Like I know if she's got a problem or, worse, gonna break down. I can't do that wearing shoes. My feet keep me in the groove with the bus so I'm connected. It was hot at first, but they've grown into it.'

'You're a bus driver?'

'I am, an' I drive a magic bus and I tell you – much

magic happens lady!'

He tapped the book on my lap.

'Ram Dass. I've gotta tell you what happened. The man has real downers – gets depressed, every time he comes down from taking acid. That's when he's still in the States. So he goes east to search for something that won't bring him down, that lasts, and he finds his teacher in India. So one day this guru asks him for some acid. He reaches out his hand and demands it, then he says, give him some more, a much higher dose than Ram Dass reckons is OK for a man over sixty. But he gives it anyway. He's a scientist, right? He's curious. So he watches Maharajji carefully and you know, nothing, but nothing happens. Maharajji is untouched. He just acts normal and then he winks at him after an hour or two. Just winks! So the joke's on Ram Dass.'

'So why wasn't he affected?'

'He was enlightened. He was somewhere else. Way beyond what drugs can do. And he saw everything. He knew Ram Dass's thoughts.'

'Wow . . .'

I looked at Zeb wondering if he took acid or if, like Ram Dass, he had found other ways to get high. Maybe his bus was his path somehow. He seemed to relate to it as if it was alive. I didn't feel any need for hard drugs. I felt high enough already. I was like an excited child discovering an imaginary world. But it was not Narnia, not something make-believe, but my inner world that was waking up.

Zeb interrupted my thoughts with a nudge.

Grinning, he said: 'Come and see my bus. You might want to join the party when I leave for Delhi next week.'

We walked out of the inn and turned down a narrow street where a multi-coloured bus was parked up against an old warehouse. It had seen better days; there were rusty holes in the paintwork, but Zeb stroked the yellow bonnet with pride.

'You said you're having a party?'

'The party, lovely lady, is on the bus. It's a trip! We all head off into the sunset together, and we party, get high, sing along, then we break down, have a laugh and sleep under the stars. There's all the hubs to stop at, get the news, buy fresh hashish, and meet everyone. We even take off on the side roads just for fun sometimes. It's a gas. It's a non-stop party all the way to India. How can you resist?!'

Zeb smiled seductively at me.

'Um, no, it sounds fantastic,' I replied, not feeling ready to accept the invitation.

'Are you full up for the next trip?

'Nearly, but there's always room for a sweet babe like you.'

I felt a bit overwhelmed by his exuberant flirting and

said I was meeting my friend. As I turned to go he grabbed my hand.

'Wait, let me just show you . . . this.'

Exuberantly, he led me round to the back of the bus. He opened the boot door with a flourish. There, beautifully arrayed, was a miniature kitchen. Cups hung on hooks, a primus and kettle were neatly stacked, cutlery in boxes screwed to the side. Large water bottles stood amongst several rolled up rubber sleeping mats.

'You see, everything you could possibly need. Fit for a princess.'

I walked to Syntagma Square full of thoughts. For a moment, standing by the brightly coloured bus in front of a huge swirling painted sunflower, I felt like getting on and spinning off to exotic places. But as I walked away from Zeb's infectious bouncing energy I realised the idea of getting on a crowded hot bus with people I didn't know felt claustrophobic. Nearing the Square I still felt the sensation of his warm hand in mine and hoped he would be around in the Outside Inn for some days. I felt enlivened by his bubbling energy and passion for life.

Not just Zeb but everyone I met glowed. There was no embarrassment about wearing your spiritual passion on your sleeve, just as Sohani had openly displayed her tears. In all my meetings and conversations there was a lack of cynicism along with a free spirit of exploration. Paths such as Buddhism, Hinduism and Sufism were hungrily followed. Books were passed round and eyes shone with a transparent desire for inner connection. The open atmosphere went with people having little money and few possessions. Materialism had depleted a sense of spirituality and the counter-culture was the reaction. Less possessiveness and living on the road also led to more interaction with local people.

Awe and wonder were real responses to a rich melting pot of spiritual ideas and experience. People were passionate for enlightenment. Everyone wanted to discover and explore deeper states of consciousness. Sharing this inspired vision, I felt part of a big, accepting, collective family living parallel to society, but within a freer more transparent one. I experienced peace and love not as empty words but actively lived. I came across acts of generosity that stunned me.

One day in the Outside Inn a traveller was playing beautifully on a very fine guitar. He ended the piece and then held the guitar out to those of us listening.

'I've travelled with this to India and back; it's time to pass it on. Who would like it?'

I felt awed by his nonchalance, how he just gave with so much ease. I stared at his calm oval face framed by his long curling hair. His offer bewildered my assumptions. I felt as if my old feelings of wanting, of always feeling I had less, were lifted out of a small hole into the light and told another story. I sensed his relaxed non-possessiveness gave him huge freedom. He showed no loss from giving away such a special possession, he just looked happy.

It was a blessing to be a hippy in 1973.

Much as I loved meeting people hot-footed from the east, I equally needed time alone. This little church was tucked away down a street nestled behind a small hill. I was peaceful and undisturbed for an hour or so drawing in my sketch book.

My little sewing kit and my sketching gave me still moments away from the intensity of countless meetings. As the climate was warm and dry I found quiet places to go in the middle of the city. I repaired my long, thin cotton skirt with oddments of pretty cloth, regaining my balance, digesting a kaleidoscope of new thoughts and ideas.

While I slipped away from the lively talk to have time alone, in contrast Izzy thrived on nonstop company. Yet we were always tuned into each other somehow, and without making any plans to meet in the day, we always did. We lived hour by hour in this buzzing city hub of countless hippie meetings and leavings, learning about the road ahead with all its choices and challenges. Any hindrances were inevitably part of the fun. Our flow was unstoppable. We had no commitments or plans and were ready to move on when we felt called.

3

Unravelling in beauty

Before we left England we'd made plans to stay on a kibbutz in Israel. I had exchanged letters with one in the east, which was expecting us. But I felt no inclination to follow our pre-arranged plans and I wasn't ready for work. The Greek islands were calling, everyone spoke about their beauty, and after five days of the city's heat and hassle we were longing to go. One evening we heard there was a ferry leaving for the island of Ios the next morning.

I went out early to buy food and was startled to see so many people on the streets. I was rarely awake at six thirty. I had arranged to meet Izzy at Piraeus, the port, but she wasn't there and the boat was leaving. I panicked, but boarded anyway and searched all over the boat for her. Finally I realised she could get the next ferry and I let my worry go. It was a test for my independence, having travelled together up to that point. But I was relieved to find her later – she'd been on the boat all along, chatting away with new friends. She assumed I would find her, which I always did.

I don't remember the rest of the journey, but I was amazed at my first glimpse of Ios. Nothing had prepared me for such stark beauty and the total change from the capital.

September 6

> *The contrast was incredible. I felt totally dazed as we arrived. A smooth blue sky, stark white moulded continuation of buildings, and the sea bringing a combination of both: deep blue with silver streaked across it. Ios seems to surpass reality. Now, the second day, I still haven't come down. Everything is very different. I feel like I've needed this for ages – I think I stayed long too long at home without a break. Went to the beach today. The heat makes everything lethargic. All's been slowed down.*

Amazed by the beauty we walked up from the little harbour and down a hill to a long beach where we would sleep, it turned out, for the next three weeks. The softly rounded low buildings dazzled us with their bright whitewash in the midday sun, all framed by the blue intensity of sea or sky. It was so peaceful after Athens. There were clusters of people on the beach around makeshift shelters, talking and playing music. Here again was a community of people we were instantly drawn to, linked by our lifestyle and our clothing. As we stepped down onto the beach a small group welcomed us and within minutes of sitting with them, life on Ios was unfurled: the best places to swim, how to avoid sea urchins, the good cafés, the locals, the hippies and the dope. At twilight I unrolled my sleeping bag out on the friendly sand. It felt familiar and natural. I didn't know when I left home that I would sleep outside for weeks on end. Discovering a passionate love for living in nature made me feel balanced and whole.

Over the following days, Izzy and I would head out each day round the headland, out of sight of the café on the beach. We joined a group of people who congregated each day on some huge flat rocks. This was my first experience of nudity. I had never imagined naked people relating to each other no differently than if they were clothed. We were both shy to start with, and took time to absorb the atmosphere. I watched how naturally the men and women related to each other. Some were English but mostly they were American or European.

I feasted my eyes on the turquoise water. The colour itself fed something inside me. There was a clarity and vibrancy as if it was a different element from the English waters I had come from.

Rob was a large, laid-back, jovial American with a loud voice and a sweet nature. Along with the others he good-naturedly encouraged us to strip off, gleefully demonstrating a leap from a high rock into the water, throwing his great bulk into space, hitting the water, then coming up laughing and spluttering.

Izzy and I wore bikinis. It took us a few days to relinquish our tops. It was a kind of initiation but no one pushed us and we took our time. On the day we finally leapt laughing into the shining sea with nothing on, a lot more than bikinis had been shed and washed away. I felt I had been reunited with nature.

I began to notice it was brief bikinis and swimwear that created titillation and sexual charge. Within our group there were inevitable attractions, yet being naked in a natural environment seemed to relax gender difference and diminish sexual tension. Nakedness created equality and ease between us; instead of the semi-naked body being so intensely sexualised it is robbed of the freedom to just be.

No one wore suntan lotion. We all felt the sun was good for us. It was later in the 70s when ozone was rapidly depleting that skin cancers began to be connected with prolonged sun exposure. Some people used tanning lotion to help them go browner but there was no awareness of any risk. I basked in the Mediterranean heat, worshipping the sun to my heart's content.

One day I glanced at Izzy. She was sitting naked on the edge of our flat rock, swinging her legs carelessly over the translucent ultramarine below. She was exquisite. An even tan covered her perfect figure and a light showering of freckles graced her face. She was talking with a German man as brown as her with long fair hair down his back. She laughed suddenly, tilting her head back, her black curls gleaming in the light. Her silver necklaces sparkled and her eternally jingling bangles chimed softly on her slim wrists. In one hand she held a roll-up – the last remaining strands of her Golden Virginia. She looked so happy, fully aware of the young man's adoring gaze – and completely unaware of her own beauty.

Like all young women we were unconscious of our comeliness. We also didn't worry how we looked. Our physical appearance was not uppermost; self-image was present, but was only one part of the whole hippie mind-set. Feeling accepted and at ease we had little self-criticism of our bodies and, living close to nature, clothes and make up weren't important. We had managed to escape the insidious lure of the advertising industry, with its insistent yet unattainable ideal of female perfection.

The food was delicious and my daily swims whetted my appetite for Greek salad, moussaka and retsina. Izzy was less interested in buying meals. One afternoon, ravenous after swimming, I arrived up at the village. Walking towards a café I was amazed to see her sitting down at a table some tourists had just left, about to tuck into the half-finished plates.

'Izzy what are you doing? They're someone's leftovers!'

Unperturbed, she gazed back at me with her round dark-blue eyes.

'Why not? We don't have much money and this will be chucked out. It's not infected, they've only just gone.'

She was an intrepid early recycler.

Each evening at 6.30pm, the Ios club on top of the hill played classical music to the setting sun. It became a ritual each day to honour the huge red orb retreating into the sea. We would walk up from the beach to the club, a tiny shack selling drinks on a circle of concrete cut into the hillside. The event drew a lot of people. To get a good view, some people climbed up on the rocks above the club to look down the valley to the sea. Everyone grew completely still as the sun dropped lower and lower. The watery horizon was splattered in reds and pinks of all shades as big speakers thundered out Beethoven's ninth symphony or Tchaikovsky's 1812. No one spoke. I looked around the hillside at figures sitting erect and still, all looking out at the sun. I felt part of a mystical experience. I had never witnessed nature being so powerfully honoured and I loved being part of something so wordless.

September 9

> *Wrote a letter home. Went to the cove later. Everything's still very unreal, but I'm feeling very happy – wallowing in the unreality…*

After years of public girls' school, living on this utterly beautiful unspoilt island was extraordinary and wonderful. I had no structure, hardly any plans, and was just hanging out and having fun. At school I had been interrogated about my future career in the headmistress's dark office surrounded by a semi-circle of stern teachers. They were like a firing squad. School was something to survive, dyslexia was unknown, and my creative strengths had been rarely noticed.

Letting my body unwind in nature I began to be myself. I was experiencing life in my own time and I could be with the journey rather than the destination as most of the spiritual teachings taught. I was reading Carlos Castaneda's "The Teachings of Don Juan: A Yaqui Way of Knowledge". I was enthralled by Castaneda's spiritual apprenticeship with his teacher. I imagined myself in his place, fully awake in all my senses and seeing other levels of reality. My inner adventure echoed my external adventure. Looking back at my excitement I see the innocence of my nineteen-year-old self, and how in fact I knew so little about spiritual practice, yet I connected to it and to nature with all the force and freshness of a young life set free.

Castaneda challenged my sense of reality; asserting it could be fluid instead of static. I had always thought seeing was believing, instead of allowing the possibility that believing could be seeing. That meant nothing was fixed, which gave me huge hope for my life after having felt such a failure at school. Castaneda rejected there being only one way to understand our physical relationship with the world and this excited me. Like him, I felt I was on a path of the heart.

Yet despite my spiritual leanings, Izzy said I was the practical one. I was the one who booked ferries, ate square meals, and thought in advance about our plans. One evening we were drinking in Ferrari's restaurant, sitting at different tables, each with various friends. I was letting go that evening, enjoying myself and not feeling responsible. Izzy walked off and I vaguely noticed her bag on the table. Perhaps I was in reaction against my responsible self, as that night I just stopped looking after her. This time I felt it was her responsibility, thinking she'd be back. When she came back in the morning it was gone.

September 12

Put up a poster proclaiming the loss of poor Izzy's possessions. She's leaving for Athens today. Will she ever get it all together?

Her bag had her passport and money in it. I felt guilty I had acted so nonchalantly and was worried, but Izzy took it calmly, didn't blame me, and two days later took the ferry to Athens to get a replacement. We never spoke about whether we'd do things together or not. Our comings and goings simply happened. They depended on what we each wanted at any given moment and who we were with. We gave each other complete freedom. It mostly worked because we had no agendas or attachments. Life happened and we responded. We rarely made plans and by talking to people in our fluid community we found out all we needed to know.

September 15

The wind was really into blowing our shelter down last night, but it was still standing above my head when I woke late. Because of sleeping so deeply I didn't know where I was when I woke up and felt really alien to Ios. Even though Izzy and I seem totally independent of each other, when she's not actually around… She is invaluable to me when it comes to meeting new people.

Izzy was the more outgoing of us two. I was shyer and missed her when she went to Athens. The changing weather was also affecting me. I knew lots of people but had no close friends and I felt lonely sleeping on the beach in the wind. Yet I don't remember wondering how long she would be. The fact we had no way of communicating was normal. I wasn't worried and just assumed she would be back soon even though she had no money or passport when she left. I was right. Izzy got herself to the embassy in Athens, replaced her passport and was back in five days.

September 16

I walked around the headland for a while. Found a church — similar to all the other little round ones in Athens. So cool and soothing inside. The woman who let me in had brought some herbs to put in a bowl. They smelt incredible. Found some deserted rocks further up. Stayed till late afternoon. Walked back to town and met 2 people. Went back for Ouzo in their tent.

There was this contrast between the wild colourful freedom of the hippies on the beaches against the ancient landscape and the women in long black dresses with their traditional customs. But despite our huge differences, the island Greeks were always warm and friendly like patient and long-suffering parents.

September 17

I almost feel attached to our old shelter despite the lack of the finer things of life! Walked up into the valley behind the beach. Found a mule's skeleton. Sat under a little tree and drew. Can get the pattern and shapes — and also develop them, but cannot get the perspective or likeness. Definitely into abstraction, but the bones have to be known first.

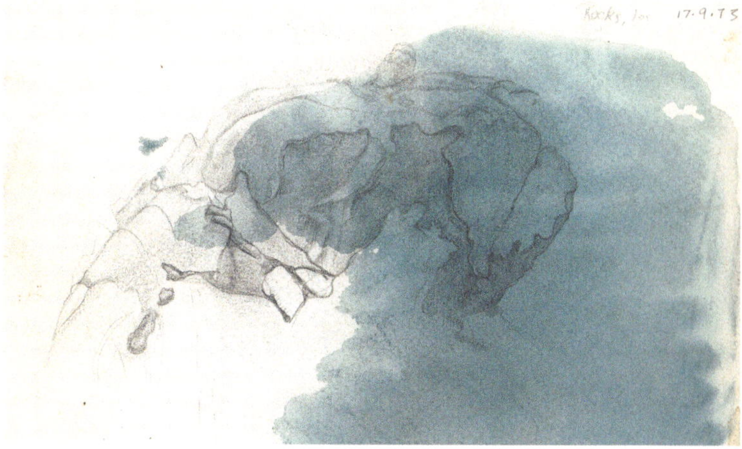

Although we were laid-back about sleeping on the beach, the Northern Meltemi winds were strengthening even more and blowing the sand around. We made a shelter out of sticks, cloth and twine, and even though it was just around our heads, it meant we could sleep without sand being blown in our eyes.

I think one of the ways my friendship worked so well with Izzy was because we shared the same levels of risk-taking and safety. We liked smoking dope but neither of us did harder drugs. We would stay up all night, but neither of us got pregnant. Even so, the next experience we had scared us.

September 19

> *We had a smoke with a little American guy who had some Afghan which was very fresh, or spiked with something. We were out of our heads for two hours. Izzy really freaked. I don't think he was quite on as he took Izzy for a walk and tried to freak her even more verbally and even more physically.*

This was our first bad experience. So far our meetings with people had flowed along in unspoken trust. We took for granted everyone's good intentions and up to this point we had been right. I remember sitting on the nearly dark beach with this man who was persuading us to smoke with him. Neither of us trusted him. I sensed Izzy was as wary as I was and we both refused, but he worked on us with the worst hippie judgement – that we were being hung-up and uptight. It worked. We ignored our intuitions because being seen as uptight was worse. We were hippies but not streetwise, and the difference made us vulnerable.

Whatever we smoked that night was horrible. After a few puffs of the joint, Izzy went off for a walk with him and I got into my sleeping bag. I lay awake in my sleeping bag feeling anxious for the first time about Izzy's safety. Hours later she returned and I could sleep. We both woke feeling dizzy and strange. Although knocked by the experience, I was relieved we were basically ok.

I inhaled less of it than Izzy and years later she said, 'You knew I was off my head and you had to keep it together.' It was in a conversation we had in our late fifties. I was surprised she felt I was protective of her. I was, in fact, but she had never before shown she was aware of this. It was good to be appreciated by her many years later.

Santorini

September 22

> *Walked up to 'Ancient Thera' with Sammy. The road wound up the mountain like a monotonous snake. The ruins were bigger and better than I expected. The view was pretty amazing. Dug a hole and found some pottery before the little guard caught me. I walked down feeling shattered in the heat. Went for a swim and tried to recover on the beach. Adrien and Marsell, two American girls drove us to the port. I feel really happy with them all. Arrived Ios about 9.00pm to find Izzy having a scene with a little Irish guy.*

I wanted a change and heard there was a ferry going to Santorini. A few hours later I was on it while Izzy remained on Ios. After living on the bright pale sand for two weeks I felt the need for a contrast and I was fascinated to hear about the black volcanic sand. After a couple of hours on the ferry I noticed an expectancy as we drew in to the island. Everyone was standing up on deck looking out as we neared the bright and peaceful harbour. I had come with three friends: a German couple and an American called Sammy. We were told by a local that the blackest beach was a few miles away so we walked out of the harbour, arriving on the beach by the evening. It was more dark grey than black and I was a bit disappointed, but it was a change. I had my little guitar and played Donovan songs as the sun set. We made little shelters of stone walls and for four days slept at the top of the beach under pine trees that dropped resin down on our bags all night. For 2 drachmas we could take a shower – a pipe sticking out of a wall with a wooden board underneath – outside a tiny café. The four of us spent the days walking, talking and sunbathing.

One afternoon I was naked on the beach with Sammy under a cloudless sky. He started throwing little stones at me. It was playful and didn't hurt, but it had an edge. The other two were out of sight. Suddenly I felt a bit unsafe, not understanding why he was taunting me. I looked at the sun-tanned bearded face next to me and realised I didn't really know him at all. We were all used to being naked together, but I was alone with him and felt exposed. Something was going on, he was saying something, but I didn't know how to ask what. I floundered in confusion and swam out into the turquoise luminosity of the sea to try to clear my thoughts. We took indirect messages as the norm and muddled through, never having learnt how to communicate in tricky interactions.

I stayed four days on Santorini and when I returned Izzy was low, as her friend was moving on. I consoled her. People were always leaving and love was usually short-lived in our mercurial lives. I took more time to get involved with people I was drawn to and so had less heartbreak, yet Izzy was never down for long. She bounced up again with the next new faces we met.

Paros

September 26

> *Revived after a swim. Walked to Pisa Levada and had some breakfast. Washed our hair under the tap. So quiet and peaceful after the rush on Ios. It's nice being a threesome. We all seem very happy. Walked to Drios, a nearby village of 2 houses in the dark. Given glasses of Ouzo and walked back.*

Izzy and I and a friend called Nick went to the island of Paros. We found an isolated beach on the other side of the island and stayed on it for three days with one trip to a tiny village for water and ouzo. We ate very little, just a tin of sardines, bread and some fruit. We were pretty much fasting though I was unaware of it.

We had the whole beach to ourselves and we each made our own private sleeping space amongst the bamboos and grass at the edge of the sand. Those few days left a lasting impression on me. I felt a deep feeling of peace, freedom and safety I hadn't felt before. We were naked for three days and saw no one. To have my largest organ, my skin, wholly in contact with the sea breezes, salt water and the sun for that long, was a rare and precious experience. I felt all my needs were met, and that I was deeply alive in a state of serene joy. Later in Israel I was given Kahlil Gibran's "The Prophet," and his words affirmed the rightness of what I experienced.

"Would that you could meet the sun and the wind
With more of your skin and less of your raiment.
For the breath of life is in the sunlight and the
Hand of life is in the wind."

In later years I saw the 1970s Australian film "Walkabout", in which two white children make their way across the outback, helped by a young aborigine. There's a scene when they come upon a beautiful water hole and swim together ecstatically. When I saw this scene I remembered being completely immersed in nature on the beach in Paros, speaking little, yet being in deep harmony with my companions.

Athens again

September 29

> *Woke up early on the beach near the Port. It began to rain. We seemed to have timed it well. Went to the cafe by the windmill and wandered round the town while it was still drizzling. It was a good change. The rain helped to clear my head. I felt pretty bad, sick, dizzy but managed to fight it off for a while. Went into Paros cathedral – meant to have 100 doors.*

Izzy and I took the boat from Parikia, the port at Paros, and left the islands for good. We were both feeling low, the weather was grey, and arriving in Athens the city drained us even more. I was grieving the loss of my peaceful immersion in nature and the metropolis, with its noise and crowds, was a jangling ordeal.

I was still feeling sick and dizzy, and after a couple of nights in The Outside Inn I made my way to the hospital. I found myself walking down a sterile white corridor assaulted by staccato heels clattering round me on the polished floor. I walked into a room and two very clean doctors in white clothes stood facing me. As I looked from one to the other I panicked. A large part of me was still on the beach on Paros. I felt like a wild animal torn out of its natural habitat.

One doctor examined me and said something was wrong with my middle ear and told me to take some pills and cream. He was formal and cool and his English was perfect, but I was stretched beyond my limits, befuddled from feeling sick and losing my sense of balance, and I collapsed and cried. On seeing me sitting head down in tears his stance softened, and he met my eyes for the first time, reassuring me the pills would help. He started relating to me as a real person, with kindness, and I felt better. He generously gave me the medicine for free. I caught a taxi back to Syntagma Square and headed straight into another adventure.

October 1

> *Sitting quietly outside American Express, 2 guys came up and asked us if we wanted a free meal. Throwing caution to the wind, we went along to find an American gambler had made a good win and invited 12 freaks out to dinner, with brandy & whiskey afterwards in his suite. It was a bit weird.*

I wrote in my diary about the accommodation, food and lifts that were given to us. I believed the world was friendly and generous and so it was. Travelling seemed to put us in the right place and right time for things to happen, including this strange occurrence. A motley assortment of hippies with ragged clothes trouped off to a plush high-rise apartment on the 15th floor with tall windows looking out over Athens. We all sat round a long dining table in a luxurious and expensive suite. The walls were covered with ornate dark wallpaper with small lamps shining down onto dark paintings that I hardly took in. We had all been chatting and laughing at our good luck as we came up in the lift, but the formality of the dark room bid us all to silence. A perfectly groomed butler in black jacket and tie met us at the door and showed us in without a word. The food was all brought to the table and we helped ourselves, still silenced by the odd atmosphere. Some people tried to make conversation but it soon dried up. Izzy and I hardly knew anyone and we felt awkward. We were anticipating the meeting with our American host, but he remained absent. After a while someone asked the butler where he was, and was told he was away on business. I wondered if that was true. Maybe he was shy, or perhaps he was watching through a peephole. Despite our earlier laughter I felt I was being given charity, as if my lifestyle was not my choice. Or I was an object, an odd sensation when my aim was to be at one with life. After being served drinks in the lounge afterwards, we were glad to get out in the sunshine again.

October 2

Decided to leave for Delphi. Went along to American Express, wrote myself a sign hoping for a ride but waited a long time. Finally Alan, who also ate last night, and Jodie an Irish girl joined me, and we spent 4 hours hassling around Athens looking for a bus. Eventually we took a bus to Daphne and hitched from there. We were an odd mix of people, American, Irish and English, but I felt so joyful and light. Feeling myself growing younger when I have these moods. I have to enjoy them, for they will, I think, pass. We arrived at night after really good lifts. Last one was an open truck, and Alan and I had a smoke in the back, driving through the mountains, the black rushing night going past, looking up at the stars. It was amazing. Found a YHA way past closing time and climbed in a window with the help of two Israelis. Woke at 5.00am in the morning freezing, so I wandered around the hostel and found some blankets. Then I slept better. We made our way up to the ruins and began to absorb. It was very hot but very satisfying. They were amazing ruins. Finally we found the spring and we drank and drank out of it and washed our feet and hands. Then we crossed the road and saw the sanctuary of Apollo and the gymnasium. The "Tholos" was the best. I loved its perfect circle of stones. People kept coming up with their expensive cameras and taking pictures of us! It had to be taken as a joke after a while. I ate with an American and a Canadian and afterwards had a smoke together. I got really stoned. After getting Jodie into the hostel, Alan and I (somehow?) climbed up Mt Parnassus.

I remember crawling up in the dark through the trees. There was no path, but Alan and I both felt a strong urge to leave the comparative comfort of the hostel and get up high. Finally we found a flat area and unrolled our bags. I lay in the dark hearing the wind soughing through the pine trees. Then I felt an arm slide across my body. It was a surprise. Alan had felt like a brother. He was a good friend but I didn't fancy him. I felt indignant and turned my back waiting to see if he would try touching me again, but the next thing I heard was his steady breathing as he slept. I had come for the mountain and simply wanted to experience Mount Parnassus that night. It never occurred to me he wanted more than friendship.

I'm so thankful I did climb it then, as two years later it was made into a ski resort. The untouched changeless feeling of history seeping out of the earth and rock was rare and precious to experience. I felt shocked to hear of the development taking place so soon after I was there. I felt the people and machinery would have changed the atmosphere and broken the peace.

Tourists were another breed to us. Scrubbed clean with their ironed clothes and flashy cameras they seemed unreal. We were scornful of them as they only seemed to touch the surface of things. They looked disconnected from the environment around them and from local people. They seemed to keep themselves in little bubbles, holding tight to their own culture without engaging with the reality around them. They regarded us as strange beings too. I was always uncomfortable in tourist role. It robbed me of any real contact with a country, people or place.

October 4

Woke up to a pine tree roof and a view thousands of feet down, and even further down to Itea the port, and the sea beyond. I was filled with a sense of having reached somewhere and really absorbed it completely. There's an air of so much having taken place here on Mt Parnassus. Walked down to the tourist-invaded town and bought some break-

fast – bread, jam and milk. It was a good morning. Began hitching in the hot, hot sun. Felt I wouldn't make the boat. It was about 1.30pm. But got good lifts after all. Arrived Athens 4.00pm. Izzy was as usual in a state of 'all-things-happening', but after having to persuade her to come to Israel and not Amsterdam, we got it together to leave. Said goodbye to Alan. Afterwards on the boat realised how sad I was. He wanted me to go to Lebanon to bring some dope back to Athens to sell.

The fluidity of the life I was living danced along with constant change. This flowing state provided my intuition with a fertile bed in which to be active and strong. I usually made good choices. I would never have travelled to Lebanon to buy drugs, but I was sad to leave the friends we had made in Athens. I made so many sweet connections with people I wouldn't see again. But the moments of parting in the many goodbyes were always coloured by a bigger excitement about what was coming next. I was carried along in a lively stream of people and events, heedless of borders and time. The feelings of loss I had then were much lighter than those I have now, forty years on rooted in one place. Now I'm aware of my mortality and change is less fluid.

Greek matchboxes

4

Unforeseen Events

October 5

> *Woke up having slept really well in our aircraft style seats. Day spent in playing guitar, talking, taking a shower. We stopped in Rhodos and were allowed off the boat for 4 hours. Rocking so much we felt sick. Walked round with Eddie and Hussein. Both ok people. This morning they tried to stop in Turkey but it was too rough. This evening we sat in the Range Rover – only car on board belonging to a photographer making his way to Africa – with tape dec fitted out and dope and ouzo supplied, but it got a bit too much after a while — we've become addicted to loving the basic things of life living on the islands for so long.*

On board the Apollonia en route to Haifa we headed out once more into the unknown. Our ship was no small island ferry: her wide bow pointed east to unknown waters, committed by the regular thud of the big engines driving tirelessly over the water. Within hours an easy-going camaraderie prevailed amongst the third class passengers. We were all living on one deck together and a feeling of community and openness grew between us. There were no individual cabins to retreat to, just plenty of large, comfortable reclining seats to sleep in. This informality was second-nature to Izzy and me. Soon little groups were forming and chatting and laughter filled the room. There were about thirty Western travellers and a few Greeks. As third class passengers we were all excluded from the rest of the ship apart from the open deck, where the Range Rover was strapped up near the bow. Booming out of all four wide-open doors Pink Floyd wailed across the water. There were extra big speakers fitted inside and we were all invited to sit inside and drink ouzo. I felt odd sitting in a car on top of a boat. Out through the open car door I spied a fishing boat passing slowly by in the opposite direction. The fishermen were lined up in a row on deck staring and pointing. They clearly found it strange too. I preferred to sit out on the deck playing guitar.

In the afternoon I was sitting inside watching the waves pass by the porthole. An old Greek woman sat next to me with her two friends or maybe her daughters. They wore black dresses, shiny in places with wear, with shawls around their shoulders. Around them on the floor were strewn their possessions: crates of food, bundles and baskets of clothes. I felt the older woman's eyes on me and I turned to her. She put down the shirt she was sewing in her lap, and reaching out a strong brown hand, picked up my empty coffee cup. She put the saucer on top of the cup and turned it over. When she turned it back, the coffee had run down the sides creating a miniature landscape with other shapes emerging on the saucer. She stared intently at them while I waited in anticipation, realising she was going to tell my fortune. The other two women watched silently. Finally she looked at me and pointed at a bird-like shape on the saucer. It was hawk-shaped as if hovering, then she spoke very fast in Greek with the other two chipping in, sometimes loudly disagreeing. I listened hard, but I could not follow her. I was so frustrated. I dearly wanted to know what she was saying, but she spoke no English and my grasp of Greek was too simple. She finished talking and turned to her friends — and my future remained unknown. I gazed at the fascinating black shapes curling round the sides of my cup for ages, imagining the shape of things to come, without an inkling of the morrow.

October 6

> *2.00pm today war broke out on the Egyptian and Syrian borders. Our boat is staying in Cyprus tonight until tomorrow evening. Seems it is the worse outbreak since 67'. It's really good that there's such a good crowd on board. Nobody seems to be really down about the situation. But I don't know how I'm going to stand the waiting. Freaked tonight. I think because of too many people. Can't really believe there's a war going on 15 miles away.*

Syria and Egypt had staged a surprise attack on Israel. I had no idea how serious it was, or that it could have blown into something far bigger. Arab states sent troops as reinforcements to Syria and Egypt, and an oil embargo was enforced on the West. It was the Yom Kippur war and would go on until the 25th, when the United Nations put a ceasefire in place. The boat was halted and no one was allowed off. Being stuck on the boat intensified our community. Conversations became more open and heightened discussions were had about our situation. I struggled with feelings of claustrophobia and went out to be alone on the quiet deck. Everyone inside was talking urgently, trying to find out what was happening. The intensity made me anxious, so many needs and opinions being loudly voiced. I needed clarity and calm.

October 7

> *Went along to the kitchens to score some food. Some of the stewards are really nice but the purser and chief steward are really mean considering how much food is thrown away. There's a feeling of togetherness in our little third class section of the ship. Always seems to be situations like war or great disasters that unites people. We all gave a few dracs and someone went ashore to buy some food. But after consulting lawyers we have been ripped off — they should have been feeding us. Instead we have been eating half eaten rolls from the first class passengers. They announced we are sailing to Famagusta tonight on the other side of Cyprus at 6.00pm.*

The ship stopped providing any food for us. At first everyone met this with good-natured ease as most of us ate simply anyway. But as the hours went by, the easy-going feeling in our little community turned to anger at being treated so meanly. Izzy and I had got so hungry we went off along some long narrow corridors to the kitchens to ask for left-over food. Finally our community mobilised and someone was elected spokesman and we got permission to go ashore to buy food before we left for Famagusta.

It was a relief to be on the move again and as we set out to sea I stood in the place on the boat I loved most: right up by the bow – the furthest point forwards with only a single rail between me and the foaming water beneath. None of the ferries then prohibited passengers being there. No health and safety rules existed. Looking out over the bow I felt I was dancing over the water.

I wasn't disappointed we were no longer heading for Israel. We were cruising again and my belly was full. After all the drama Izzy and I relaxed. She had joined me on the bow with our new friends Eddie and Pierre. We all stood watching the prow of the boat slicing through the warm Mediterranean sea, which turned darker and darker shades of turquoise as the light fell. Just below our feet the white ebullient foam bubbled out from under the bow, staying bright long after the sea had gone black. Pierre passed a joint and then began a chant and as we joined in I felt a serene bliss, a deep level of peace that gave me the feeling I was expanding out in front of the boat to the horizon. That blissful feeling is still vivid; my body leaning against a huge anchor as we sung Indian Sanskrit chants together for hours through the night.

'Govinda Jaya Jaya, Gopala Jaya Jaya

Radha Ramana Hari, Govinda Jaya Jaya.'

October 8

Slept on the deck last night again. So much fresher but woke up cold with the wind blowing down my sleeping bag. Apparently the ports are all closed again after being open all yesterday. A representative from each country went ashore to appeal to the consul. Our alternatives are to return to Piraeus, paying; stay in Cyprus until a boat or plane is available, or possibly persuade the captain to sail (once the port opens) Everyone except him wants the boat to go on. A petition sent round obviously made that clear.

That afternoon after arriving in Famagusta there was a loud announcement on the loudspeaker.

'Attention! Miss Isabel Flynn and Miss Caroline Born to come to the Captain's Office immediately.'

Izzy was sitting with some friends across the room. My head jerked up to meet her eyes. We both jumped to our feet and walked towards each other as the loudspeaker called our names again.

'What on earth is going on?'

'God knows. Why us? What's he want us for?'

I was in a panic as we took off down the corridors. On the way there I quickly flushed my very small lump of dope down the loo. This was a sudden, startling demand from authority.

Col Avery, high up in the UN in Cyprus, had arrived with instructions from Izzy's parents to take her off the boat… Eventually after much freaking I went with Izzy. The Apollonia is due to sail back to Athens tomorrow. Driven off in a black chauffeur-driven Mercedes with messages coming in on the radio. Col contacted head office to phone his wife to expect us… Arrived in Nicosia… such total extremes of living – one minute on the boat begging and scrounging, then at a dinner table trying to adjust.

Izzy's parents had decided it was too dangerous for their daughter to be stranded with a war raging, and insisted she return to England. They had contacts in the UN, thus the reason we were whisked off the boat. Everything happened so fast. After being driven through the dark to the Colonel's luxurious home we suddenly found ourselves at a posh dinner table conversing politely.

'So, girls . . . ', Colonel Avery looked across the table at Izzy, 'what have you been doing in Greece?'

'Um, it's . . . been . . .', Izzy answered, looking very disconcerted, giving me a little sideways grimace, a message for help. I leapt in:

'Oh we had a lovely time in Athens staying with a friend near the Acropolis and then we visited the islands. It's been wonderful.'

Izzy followed suit. Despite our hippie language, we knew this one well. I saw her compose her face in an instant and draw herself up.

'Oh yes, a super time. The best thing was the club on Ios. They played Tchaikovsky with drinks at sundown. Everyone went.'

The colonel pursed his lips: 'Isobel, your mother has been worried, there's only been one letter.'

But Izzy had found her feet. Ignoring his last comment she continued to eloquently describe hippie life as a bohemian existence they surely must realise every young thing should be doing.

After the initial culture shock sitting at the table, we both shifted gear to the familiar so-called sophisticated banter, but I felt like a chameleon, so quickly adapting to the language and decorum needed, as if living rough on the beaches had never happened.

They had a daughter a couple of years younger than us, who appeared the next day in school uniform. She seemed to be from another generation, how we had been a very long time ago. She stood quietly in the room as we chatted, not knowing how to relate to us. That day Izzy was torn between staying and going home. Clara, the Colonel's wife, was supportive and sympathetic to her plight, and we spent a few days trying to work out what to do, all the while being generously entertained. The next day Clara drove us to Kyrenia Castle. I was relieved to get out and about.

October 9

I persuaded Izzy to look round the old castle. We began to talk to the people at the door. They were sympathetic and told us we could sleep on the beach and offered us work. In the castle I was aware of such a strong clash the whole time – I was trying to absorb the place while she was talking, unaware. The differences between us are so unnecessary – we both have a right to our feelings, ideas, belief's, etc.

I was feeling irritated again, and my friend, my best mate, was the focus, although she had done nothing. The recent events had been so dramatic and non-stop I needed some quiet space to reflect and replenish myself. Without it, I got moody and resentful. Izzy, in comparison, talked to digest her experience. I hadn't travelled enough to know that travelling is a huge challenge to friendship. Differing needs arise more frequently, often leading to conflict. Considering that, we mostly flowed along together very well.

We found a sunken Byzantine chapel and sat and let it all filter into our heads. We began to sing "Hari Hari Ganga" a chant that came to us, and I saw a shadow flickering on the floor. After some time we stopped because we heard the rain coming down – it was raining for the first time in a year. We walked outside and people walked past telling us this. We felt vaguely dazed and the guy who had talked to us earlier on the door turned up telling us he had an empty house if we wanted it. I don't know now. Writing it down I am aware of being more sceptical of the events that passed us that afternoon, but I still believe that the chant we sung had a lot of power and it had a strong connection to the rain.

As we walked around the ancient castle I noticed a little low circular stone building half buried in the earth. We bent down to get through a low doorway and sat on the earth floor cross-legged in the darkness. I felt cocooned in the enclosed space with just the shaft of light coming through the doorway and felt myself relaxing. It was cool and still and I said to Izzy, 'Let's chant'. Half way through our chant – that we were unwittingly singing to a sacred river in India – we heard shouts and voices outside. Long awaited rain had begun to fall. As we came out people were walking past hurriedly, smiling and talking. Someone told us excitedly how long it had been since the rain had come. Izzy and I walked away from the chapel in silence. Although often excited by the idea of synchronicity, experiencing it was strangely shocking.

October 10

The day began clear but soon got complex. Izzy's parents say she has to come home in a week. She refuses to fly and at first refused to go at all. She seems to be torn apart between hurting them and going her own way. Eddie from the boat rang. There's a plane going to Israel in 3 days. But the war gets more serious every day. Both sides claim to be winning... It seems it's my turn to make decisions. Latest decision: Izzy has resigned herself to going home on the magic bus. Staying here for her birthday first on the beach where

Eddie and some others have gone to stay.

The Colonel's wife Clara cooked us delicious meals, took us sightseeing, and gave us presents of Palestinian scarves when we left. I felt awkward being given so much. I also didn't realise she enjoyed our company. I just saw her then like one of my parent's friends, rather than another woman enjoying spending time with us. I thought the giving was one-way.

A beach on Cyprus

11 October

The realisation of how good it was to be with everyone again came slowly as we came onto the beach. A rectangular field next to a long beach with clear lukewarm water. A full clear beautiful moon that rose at 6.00pm small and orange from the top of the sea. We all slept in an army dug out with Eddie and Pierre, John, and Pete and Celia from South Africa and their baby. It was cramped, but an amazing home was hole! We went into town and found out about flights. This evening we made a fire and cooked rice and vegetables. We all felt so close. There was such a strength of togetherness around the fire in the evening.

We heard from Eddie that five people and a baby had left the boat and moved onto a beach near the port. After being pampered with hot showers, soft beds and haute cuisine in Clara's large and airy home, we joined them. I soon felt a feeling of belonging and thought nothing of leaving the luxuries behind. The Apollonia had turned round to head back to Athens and the eight of us fell into a spontaneous well-organised little community. We had all unexpectedly found ourselves on Cyprus: Izzy and I called off the boat by worried parents, others preferring to wait out the war on an island.

As I dropped back into the rhythm of living close to nature, I felt a deep love for it. It was better than all the material luxury. There was one small café at one end of the beach, and an old army bunker in the middle which we made our base, affectionately calling it "hole". There was an English man called John. His camera was permanently hooked over his shoulder. When I commented on its very tatty state, he explained he had deliberately scratched and dented it to make it less appealing to thieves on the long journey he had recently taken to India and back.

An intimacy was created between the eight of us living together on the beach for seven days. We brought the sharing and equality that had formed on the boat with us, and I lived more self-sufficiently than I had ever experienced before. Someone borrowed some dented old pans from the café, and we pooled money to buy vegetables from the nearby port. We washed the vegetables in the sea and chopped them up on a big flat stone. Celia was competent and relaxed. She cut veg with one hand, holding Daisy on her breast with the other. Others collected wood for the evening and the fire would be built up. Heaps of fresh vegetables were stirred over the flames while the rice bubbled, and when done the food was left to cool a little. Sitting round in a circle we ate with our fingers, quietly, with people calmly waiting their turn. Despite the basic conditions, there was a dignity in the manner in which we all ate from the same pot.

We took our cue from Pierre. He was a French Armenian who had been on the road longer than any of us and was well practised in living on little. He led by example, demonstrating that dignity and awareness could exist anywhere. He became a strong presence in the group and spoke in low earnest tones about the imperative of being skilled enough to live like this.

'Eet ees essential', he warned us slowly and clearly in his thick French accent.

'Xhees society ees breaking down. If we can live on leettle, zhen we weell survive. It ees self-suffeeciency wheech will save us.'

Eddie, a little bearded American, had similar beliefs, and the two of them became close buddies, talking late into the night together by the fire.

> *Woke up feeling shattered after not sleeping very well. Lay inside the shelter all morning. It was really soothing; dark and cool and still. I had slept in the field that night because I had felt claustrophobic in the shelter. Everyday we go over and over the same question of how to get to Israel even though I feel so happy here. And slowly, slowly the old feeling arose in me for someone – prompted by his small attentions. I can't put it into words really, but everything seems changed recently, becomes different every day.*

I fell in love with Pierre. I floated around in a state of bliss. Everything I did, everything I touched, was infused with a kind of gentle ecstasy. Pierre returned my quiet adoration with intense, brown silent eyes. He had a subtle charisma and was story-rich with travellings. He had taught Izzy and I the chant we sang on the bow of the boat on our last evening's sail, that made me feel so euphoric. He had long red hair swept back from his olive-brown face. Despite not being very tall he always appeared to have height, standing with head held up, always slightly one step back from the crowd, looking on with a deeply serious expression. He spoke intensely about Armenian politics and was proud and defiant. He wore long flowing shirts and a shawl thrown around his shoulders in varying shades of chestnut brown.

October 15

> *Today I walked and walked along the sand with Celia carrying Daisy. Celia seemed so young in some ways – simple and idealistic, yet she's had a lot to go through and in many ways come out unflawed. We collected shells in accepted silences while Daisy slept in the sand.*

I was blissed out on that beach. It was a mixture of falling in love as well as feeling a kinship and loving inclusion in the group. Eddie and Celia and their six-month-old baby had come from South Africa. I liked Celia's smile. She seemed to radiate happiness and managed the care of her child with incredible ease in such a basic environment. She told me she had been ill and had left South Africa because of the conflict. I see her clearly, walking along the beach naked with Daisy in her arms with her shaven head, her huge breasts top-heavy above her slim body. She would run laughing with joy in a funny crooked line as her breasts swung wildly from side to side. I had never seen or met anyone like her before. Despite my weighty summing up of her in my diary, I was for sure the less experienced one. I see now the great freedom she had inside herself.

One cool night all eight of us were sleeping in the bunker. Our bodies were packed together within the confines of the four concrete walls. There was a rustling in the darkness and a movement against my side and then light fingers stroked my face. It was Pierre. I was excited and nervous. He had turned over and was stroking me. His hand moved down to my shoulder. He wanted to make love, to express what he felt about me physically. I had never fallen in love like this, taken over by a force of joy. But here and now? I was shy and inexperienced. People were lying right up close, awake or asleep. I was painfully torn, so conscious of others nearby and I couldn't respond. Making love with bodies close on either side of me felt far too public. I needed privacy, but Pierre didn't.

I don't think Pierre was used to being rejected. The next morning when we met on the beach his eyes were level and cool. He flung his tawny shawl over his shoulder with his usual animal grace, and strode on. Nothing was said between us.

I had no fluency at nineteen to speak about the risky raw territory of intimacy, let alone any language. Neither had it dawned on me I might negotiate around love and sex. I knew nothing. The brief and painful moment washed by in the drift of days on the beach, but not from memory. It took me years of shy encounters to learn to identify and communicate my feelings and needs. At the time I went on blindly being in love with Pierre, and meanwhile life was exciting and unexpected as usual.

> *This evening we met Andreas and friend who took us out to a disco. Pete drove the car – and must have been out of his head on Morning Glory seeds from eating them in the morning and nearly killed us all... We went to Salami's Bay Hotel to a clockwork orange type disco... I danced a bit and was happy with Pierre. Izzy got freaked out by Pete and said he had strong hypnotic powers and there was a feeling of witchcraft about him. It was a strange evening; emotions on all sides got complex mingling into each other. There was a feeling of powerful awareness from every head. I was filled with happiness in my blindness... Today we went to the town like many other days and hassled round about lifts to Israel. But all was a bit fruitless. We went to the Turkish quarter and bought food and ate lunch in the moat before the old wall. Two Turkish men in an empty tavern invited us to join them for some Cyprus brandy. We all sung and played and got drunk all afternoon.*

I was in a rare flow of life with no obstacles or responsibilities. I had no worries and little conception of danger. The risk of dying or being injured from the wild driving didn't enter my mind. I had such a different relationship with my mortality. I had an innate natural trust that life bestowed kindness and good will, and within the context of the counter-culture I was in, consuming alcohol and dope with people I didn't know felt normal. I didn't see them as strangers. From other perspectives I could be seen as degenerate, but I was free, and it was freedom that mattered, along with an assumed equality with the locals. Only when danger stared me forcibly in the face was I scared, as it did months later in Turkey.

Izzy and I were breaking away from all the rules and expectations we felt constricted by. We walked into experience after experience with open arms. From a sheltered upbringing my eyes were opened wide to life and I grew up fast that year. I sang "Me and Bobby McGee", relishing how the words affirmed how free I felt from having so few possessions.

Like most teenagers I believed I could release everything, that all my past conditioning could be dismantled by a year of hippiedom. However naive, I experienced a great sense of freedom by believing this – by believing I was free. Although I had places in both art college and university, I felt bound by nothing.

The last evening on the beach we washed up as usual in the sea. John and I stood immersed knee-deep, chatting as we washed bowls and pans, letting them float beside us in the calm water. Busy with our task we had forgotten our nightly visitor. Suddenly, in front of us, there was a tiny sliver of yellow-gold, peeping at first over the line of horizon, then flooding its beauty across the sea.

Mesmerised, we stood watching while the bowls clinked softly together, the gentle sound accompanying the arrival of the huge yellow orb sailing up into the sky.

October 17

> *Left the beach. I felt it would be the last time I would be there somehow. Pete and Daisy and Celia were hard to say goodbye to. We started hitching. Got quite good lifts, arriving in Limassol really happy. We found a cafe and bought soup and wine and entertained our guests all evening. It was a crazy drunken evening. Izzy got so drunk and we were offered £30 each so two dirty old men could see some action. We found our churchyard and fell asleep after deciding not to sleep in a bus.*

John had told me about a cargo ship going to Israel and I said I'd go. But my emotions were in flux, and I changed my mind, pulled by Pierre who now spoke about going to Greece. He and Eddie seemed excitingly different, often in passionate discussion about society being on the brink of collapse and I had fallen into a foursome with him, Eddie and Izzy. I felt so enamoured with Pierre I could have followed him anywhere. John left to board the boat for Israel and I didn't think I'd meet this quiet and thoughtful man again. As we left the beach that evening, there was a wildness between the four of us as if we were fiercely flexing our wings for the next adventure.

Late that evening two old Greeks in the café offered us, or rather offered the men, this money. I was repulsed;

being paid to be watched having sex was a twisting of beauty, something I had never come across or considered. Eddie and Pierre were enthusiastic about it, but even though we were drunk, Izzy and I were adamant it was not our scene. The two Cypriot men were greasy and creepy and we walked to a churchyard in the dark to sleep.

October 18

> *This morning on waking, we were given sandwiches of bread, salad, cheese, and milk by a little Greek girl who was one of a group of children gazing at us when we woke up. She seemed sad this was the last morning we were there. Izzy and I talked in a tiny back street cafe for a long time. I wrote some more verses to her song after she left – 500 miles away from home. It was a good talk and really brought us together. I went on to the mosque and a little man showed me round, pointing the way up to the minaret. I really seemed to get a lot further in my meditation. The others joined me there.*

Izzy and I spoke affectionately to each other that morning. We knew our time together as a travelling duo was nearing an end for she would soon be on the Magic Bus heading home. I left the café wanting to visit the mosque before I left and despite our drunken evening the night before, my meditation was sweet and clear as a bell.

I had discovered mosques in Cyprus while staying with Clara in Nicosia. I had been wandering around the Turkish quarter and walked into one for the first time and felt nourished by the still atmosphere. In this one in Limassol, standing under the high circular dome, space and light were cupped into concentrated stillness and I was stopped in my tracks. The huge empty space was full of beauty and presence as if the roundness of the roof was honing energy down on top of me. I stared down at the beautiful floor covered in deep red woven carpets laid diagonally across to opposite corners. A dark little man appeared and welcomed me with a broad smile. He told me the carpets were over four hundred years old and at sunset a bell would ring and everyone could eat as the fast would end. I had come at the festival of Ramadan.

Each time I went into a mosque I was welcomed. The atmosphere would hold me in a peaceful embrace and I always dropped easily into meditation. I wasn't interested in the religious practice, I just wanted to sit there and was always left alone to do that. That day in Limassol I didn't feel any incongruity between my drunken and my spiritual states. They often followed close together and hangovers didn't dampen my spirituality. Maybe the mix of these experiences aided me in letting go into an open state of mind. I was immersed in the atmosphere of the time: an openness to explore with whatever was available.

5

A tourist no more

October 20

Arrived early in Athens from Cyprus and collected our small refunds for the ticket from Cyprus to Haifa. Athens was incredibly depressing, even more so because of having to turn back from an uncompleted mission after everything seeming to point to Israel: the I Ching, and the general state of mind I was in – really strong and purposeful.

My first time in Athens had been all excitement: at the crossing point of routes in all directions, to and from faraway places. I met people who woke me up, shook up my expectations and astonished me with their lives. As I listened to their stories, tight cloisters seemed to open up in my mind and I saw that life offered far more choices than I had thought possible. On Ios I dropped deep into my body, replenishing all the dry and barren school years with the sensual blessings of its island beauty.

This third return to Athens, following the second one after the islands, was hardest. I walked tentatively along the pavements inches from hurtling cars, the noise and fumes splintering my peace. My body's sensitivity was shocked and I hated being back. But Athens was the gateway to everywhere: the place to get boats, trains and flights, and I had no choice but to return after our aborted trip to Haifa. I needed to make some money and we had been told blood was needed in Athens. I sat in the plain, bare room in the blood bank for hours, only to discover my blood type was not needed that day. I was told I had perfect blood pressure, though that statement of good health meant nothing to me then. I took for granted my body's healthy resilience to my erratic life.

Izzy was sitting outside the American Express in Syntagma Square still vacillating about whether to go home. A man stood up and waved a return ticket to Gatwick in the air. His name was Pete Silver and he was giving it away. The dare-devil in her responded – and she took it. We said a hurried goodbye and she went to Athens airport and boarded the plane that day. She arrived in cold, wet Gatwick in a thin shirt, sarong, and bare feet. She had no money and shared a taxi with people she had been sitting with on the plane, then walked a good many miles further to friends in West Hampstead. She was in shock and didn't stay long, especially after an unfriendly meeting with her parents. A few weeks later she came to Crete.

I didn't miss Izzy. My new friendships made me feel part of a travelling community and I felt more on my own two feet. I felt very different to when she left me on Ios to get a new passport. I had formed a connection with Eddie and Pierre on Cyprus, and on the move again

I felt independent and strong.

From people we spoke to about Israel, travelling there was still dubious and I was in no hurry to go. In the cafés in Syntagma Square we heard talk of a large Greek island named by travellers as "Little India". This was Crete, the favoured place for folk returning from India as it was so laid back. On its southern coast was a village called Matala where Joni Mitchell had lived. The three of us felt drawn to go, and at 5.30am the next morning we left on a boat for Iraklion, the main port of Crete, together with a couple called Ron and Ann. Once there, after trying to hitch a lift for two hours, we all split up and I got a ride the whole seventy-five kilometres to my destination.

October 21

> *Matala was really soothing. I sat in the sun and then swam while Eddie went to look for his friend Blake. We all crashed in his house that night and ate on the roof with the sky like a black dome above us. It was so rich there with nature and beauty and millions of unwritten words, waiting.*

Matala was exquisite. It was a tiny village laid around a crescent-shaped bay. Large artificial caves had been made in the soft stone during the Neolithic Age. They became famous in the 1960s when Joni Mitchell lived in one and wrote her song "Carey" about her Greek lover with flaming red hair.

I stood on the beach and looked up at the pale, sand-stone cliffs curving out to sea at strange angles and saw caves of all shapes and sizes overlooking the water. There were a few weathered, dirty hippies moving around the cliff side. They were dour and unsmiling, sitting outside the entrances as if to ward off intruders. Any ideas I had of living there vanished. In an interview with "Rolling Stone" in early 1971 Joni Mitchell described how the hippies living in the Matala caves in the fifties and sixties were wearing necklaces of human teeth as the caves contained so many ancient skeletal and other burial remains.

For me the caves felt stale and unexciting and I turned back into the tiny village. I found "Mama's Café" and bought delicious sheep's milk yogurt with a thick yellow crust, which came in brown ceramic bowls that you washed and returned. I stood by the counter in the street a few yards from the beach spooning the cool, delicious yoghurt into my mouth. It was like nectar, such a different quality from Athens's tourist food.

Blake lived in the middle of the village and everyone knew him. He had known Eddie from the States. He was the only person renting a house in Matala as everyone else lived on the beach or in caves. In his two rooms he had a large collection of drums and books and his door was open to anyone who needed a place to sleep or something to eat. Over the weeks in Crete I went there often for food and solace. He was immensely generous, but I didn't take that in then, having grown accustomed to a culture that took it for granted that those who had more gave to those with less. We had many good conversations and I loved browsing through his art books.

One was a big colourful book of mandalas. It was the first time I had come across the idea of an image to focus on for meditation. They were big and beautiful images. The flower below I drew from that book, carefully copying it into my sketchbook. Blake's house was a sanctuary, a place I could relax in. I hung out on my own there and had time to give slow and careful attention to detail.

October 22

It took a long time to hitch to Timbaki but it was a beautiful road and we were happy. We arrived quite late and found a job for the morning quite easily. We slept outside the police station in a concrete yard.

After that peaceful first night, life on Crete was harsh. I lost a chunk of my wide-eyed wonder and had tough times physically and emotionally. I shifted even further away from anything resembling a tourist. I was definitely no longer on holiday. My money had run out and I needed to work to eat and probably pay rent. We heard that work was going in Timbaki weeding and picking vegetables, and the three of us travelled there with an American called Beth who was also skint. It was an unattractive town surrounded by low fertile land and we would be working alongside Cretans – people who knew hard work.

The following weeks were testing for me. I felt lonely at times, and the challenges I encountered impelled me to reach out to spirit for help, not the first time by any means. My life in Timbaki was tough, maybe the toughest experience in my life so far. My diary was pivotal. Between the tiny pages was a secret space to lay down my inner turmoil, that I alone was witness to.

But in a letter home to my parents I wrote:

I think maybe the war diverting me to Crete was for a reason, or certainly I don't feel I must fight against it or try to return to my original plans.

In the evening after we arrived we asked in a café for work, and a mother and her two daughters approached us and said we could work for them. The next morning we rose at five. As we walked to work, a full, strong, female voice suddenly swept past me, filling the field with melody. It was Beth. My chest lifted in response, her voice a joyful glow in my head. She had a powerful voice and I felt supported by it. Early mornings were painful wrenches for me, but on hearing her sing I breathed deeper, and my footsteps lightened in the coolness of the morning. She knew a large repertoire of Joni Mitchell and James Taylor songs which erupted regularly from her confident American lips.

Bending down weeding tomato plants for hours was back breaking. That first morning's work was a jolt to my system. My protected middle class upbringing had not acquainted my body with anything close to that kind of hard labour. Yet as I sweated under the hot Cretan sun my mind cleared. At midday the family brought us an enormous pan full of pasta, rice and meat, plus a bottle of retsina, which felt like a gift from heaven. I was so relieved to rest. Pierre was unfazed, peasant strength ran in his limbs. Beth was a tall, strong west-coaster, also much fitter than me. Only Eddie was quiet when we stopped, and I sensed he was as unused to physical labour as I was. Nothing was said about the toughness of the job. Pierre held the moral level and no one risked showing any weakness.

We ate quietly together and I watched the flies settle and crawl on the Cretan's brown-skinned limbs and faces. I couldn't stop looking, fascinated at how they completely ignored them. Later on they asked us back to their house, plied us with more food and wine, and we caroused together till dark with the family playing bouzouki and singing. All the Cretans were consistently generous to us. They lived poor and simple lives, but they laughed easily and gave us a lot. They knew very little English but laughingly told us when we said we were tired, "Healthy body, healthy mind" – the ancient Greek holistic understanding.

October 24

> *We crashed quite early in the same cold yard of concrete as last night – waking at some mad hour to the same noisy dawn chorus. I was split up from Pierre and Eddie and put to work thinning down tomato plants near the sea with Antoine. At my lunch hour I walked down the few yards to the beach and sat alone amidst the roar and shingle eating sunflower seeds, olives and bread.*

I had joyously acclimatised to living on beaches, but I struggled sleeping in a police front yard in a town. While still dark the dawn chorus woke me with a brutal cacophony of roosters and small birds, an omen perhaps of the day to come. I struggled to get going in the half-light as we were to meet our new boss, a local land owner who was offering us a few days' work. He had several polytunnels in the area growing tomatoes and cucumbers. This first morning he split us up to work in different locations. He directed the others to work in various fields near the town and then indicated to me to get up behind him on his big old noisy motorbike. I twisted my long skirt up round my legs and jumped on. We motored along sandy tracks beside the hot fields and arrived at a long polytunnel by a beach. He showed me how to thin the small cucumber plants, but soon realised I was too impatient and made too many mistakes, and told me to weed instead. After telling me to take it easy, and also, for some reason, not to go on the beach, he roared away to see to his other crops.

I ignored him. After working for a couple of hours I was hot and made for the water. It was a long stretch of empty sand curving for miles around a large bay. Way over in the distance I saw little white houses perched close to the water. They were tiny blobs, too far away to see anyone. I spent a peaceful hour swimming and eating.

As I got up to leave, a man approached. He was not much taller than me. He gestured to me to come over and talk.

I walked a few yards back down the beach to him and he asked me how much I earned. I told him and thought nothing of it, but noticed his face was impassive. I turned to head back up the beach but the next second found myself face down in the sand. He had jumped onto my back and was pinning me down. It was so sudden and surprising it was almost funny. The physical sensation in my back reminded me of my brother tripping me up as a joke. But seconds later he rolled me over and began tearing off my clothes. As he ripped off my long hippy skirt and grabbed at my pants a wave of rage swept through me and I began to shout. I wasn't screaming, I was shouting. I strangely didn't feel frightened. My voice suddenly became an instrument of power and vitality. It was as if something I didn't know I owned was suddenly mine. It surprised me to hear this unknown roar, and it surprised him.

It was at first inconceivable to me that he was trying to rape me and took me a few seconds to take it in. Then the volume of my rage increased. I began shouting, 'Police!', leaning towards the direction of the little houses. Amidst the physical struggle and emotion there was an eerie moment when we met eye to eye. Rage in mine and suddenly in his small brown eyes, fear. Then his hold weakened. Worry perhaps, of repercussions of my fierce will to alert the authorities. He went limp and I leapt away. I turned back and his face drooped into a sulk as he lay looking up at me. But my anger was not spent by any means. I went on shouting and swearing at him as I stood there. I felt an unstoppable fury. He had unwittingly released a nineteen-year torrent of backed-up anger. All the repressed years of being nice, good and obedient had finally been given cause to erupt.

I couldn't actually run from that man until I had shouted

and sworn at him in a rage. It's weird, but I think that little incident got rid of more of my frustration than his... Afterwards although I was shaken, I was filled with a tremendous energy resulting from what? I weeded in the heat for two hours in the midday sun – inside the polytunnel...! Antoine arrived to find me completely drenched through in sweat.

Antoine looked shocked when he saw me. I must have looked very changed. He was worried when I told him I had worked through the hottest part of the day inside the polytunnel and scolded me, telling me I was crazy. But I felt energised and clarified somehow, as if I had sweated out some old toxin. Later the others asked if something had happened. Beth looked at me questioningly, holding my gaze. I knew she knew something had happened to me but I couldn't speak about it. It was enough for my body and mind to digest. I was deeply shaken and needed time to unravel and not get engaged with their reactions. The intensity of the experience was of another order. I had met someone else that day: a furious Caroline I didn't know. Some molten rage had exploded, giving me indomitable strength. I discovered the power of my voice and found it to be an ally and a protector with more power than my physical strength.

October 25

Cloudy mountains, sage tea and house warming. This morning we found our house – 300 drachmas a month with running water and a loo. At first I felt a big anti-climax after seeing the house. Stupidly my idealistic little head had built the idea up much bigger.

We had been asking around for a place to rent. But when we found it I was disappointed and judged myself for dreaming of better. It was one small room for the four of us with an outside toilet across a yard. We walked from the bright street into darkness. I could just make out a dusty concrete floor from the dull light through the tiny window. But we took it, and despite the initial let down we all felt energised and set to getting the place more habitable if not homely.

We went out to find bamboo, which we cut and made into shelves and attempted to make pipes to play on. However basic, it was a base after having no fixed abode. It was also the first place I had ever rented and the first time I had paid rent. Three hundred drachmas was less than fifty pence. I was still confused by the change of pounds, shillings and pence to decimalisation two years earlier and was still adjusting to the value of drachmas. But I didn't need to know their exact worth as the rent was cheap, as was everything in Greece. Despite being so primitive, I felt some sense of ownership and belonging. The four of us seemed to have fallen in together and things improved that day.

I wrote home:

It's not a question of gathering enough energy together to get to Israel because a kibbutz can be created anywhere.

October 27

Worked with Spiro. He came along with a morning break of cakes and pomegranates soon after we had started work. He was a good boss. At lunchtime he brought Feta as well. The flies were bothering me. I felt ugly and guilty from the vibes given off by Charley when I swept them away from me again and again.

We met Spiro in the café late the previous evening and he offered us work. His field was a short walk from the town and I was quiet as we walked there, glad to be with the others again. But by lunchtime the flies were relentless and, still churned up from my assault the day before, I felt invaded and irritated by them endlessly crawling over my skin. I swore under my breath as I tried to wave them away.

Pierre, watching me, shook his head disapprovingly and I felt a failure. He had been exhorting us to love everything, assuring us that insects would then leave us alone, and love would return manyfold. He and Eddie said you had to completely drop the ego to be on a true spiritual path, and killing anything was wrong. He impressed upon me an authority of spiritual know-how, and idolising him as I did, I believed he was right. My tendency to judge myself got enmeshed in his beliefs. Without Izzy to talk things through I lost my balance. I was a woman still blindly in love, unaware how caught in projections I was or how little I was getting from Pierre that actually nourished me.

I had come from a strong downpour of theology from my father who had turned passionately to Christian Science a few years earlier. The idea was that we were all perfect reflections of God or "Perfect Mind". If you had any negativity or any physical ailment it meant you had fallen away from this understanding and needed to work at changing your lower consciousness into something much purer and higher. They were heady metaphysical ideas. Later in life when I came to celebrate my body in movement and dance as my be-all in life, his ideas were way too purist and mind-based. But at nineteen I was drawn by his enthusiastic discoveries and found them a support.

In a letter sent to my father I wrote:

> *I felt ill this afternoon but instead of letting myself drown in self-pity as I usually do, I tried to put the last few words in your letter into reality. Material sympathy only weakens, spiritual sympathy in the form of strength has so much more healing properties.*

I was seeing any physical weakness as an obstacle to be lifted out of by the power of spirit. If anyone had suggested to me my body was sacred in its own right I would have found it totally self-indulgent. I think I was also open to my father's ideas because Christianity was loosening somewhat around the world. Its mainstream fixity was shifting in America as the Jesus movement took off. Arising from a charismatic Christian renewal in which speaking in tongues, miracles, faith and healing were central, it was another groove of the hippie counter-culture rapidly sweeping across the States. Jesus freaks called for a return to simple living and rejected the church. Many lived in communes. Much music of the time cited Jesus. The rock opera Jesus Chris Superstar portrayed Jesus as an enlightened hippy and I was drawn to the lively rhythms of Christian and gospel rock, but no further. The occasional Jesus freaks I met were too evangelical.

Pierre's beliefs had a similar idealism as my father's, but Pierre was cooler. The coolness that had so attracted me was a coldness I was blind to. His grace and poise fascinated me; I had never met anyone who lived on the road in such style. He owned an elegance that made him seem rich and he was incredibly attractive. But I could not see his lack of compassion.

October 29

> *We all worked for Spiro again today. He gave us some jam and a cabbage. We were all happy once again working and Beth sang. We returned to lots of newcomers in Timbaki looking for work. This evening I was so happy with no worries, but then I needed mental space – which was strongly linked to physical space. I felt a horrible sense of claustrophobia when that need for my space wasn't able to be met by the action of another.*

In the middle of the night in our little square room Beth spoke out loud. Her quiet words were all too clear:

'Yes, Pierre yes, yes, touch me there . . . You are such a

great lover.'

I lay rigid, hardly breathing. Eddie and I, silent in our separate corners were listening, conscious of everything in the darkness. The two of them had been getting closer since we arrived in Timbaki, but I was unprepared for this blatant broadcast. I lay staring into the darkness, unable to take in what I was hearing, my mind spinning in chaos. The freedom of her love-making shocked me. I was as free as her in many ways, but her sexual directness went beyond anything I knew. It was a wretched night, as I tried to make my breath sound as if I was sleeping. Being forced to witness Beth making love with Pierre was so agonising I couldn't name it in my diary, only managing an oblique reference. I wanted to be as easy-going as her. I didn't want to accept how sensitive and sheltered I was in comparison, even though the situation was excruciating.

October 30

Eddie and I walked into town looking for work. Two Greek women approached us and said we could work for them for six hours for 90 drachmas and food. We walked all the way to their field and were fed four times altogether! They were mother and daughter and were really poor but had a great sense of humour. We laughed and worked and were taken home to eat at their house where we spent more mad hours. It was really good. It was the first time I felt I really understood the Greeks, having good communication as we accepted their hospitality. Steve and companion made their appearance later in the evening with guitar. They were really nice people but they left the next day.

It was awkward with Eddie. We both knew the other had heard the raw intimacies in the night and we avoided eye contact. Yet the constellation of the group had changed and we were strangely thrown together by Beth and Pierre's union, as well as in the necessity of work that only the two of us took on that day. But as the day unwound, with my hands in the earth in the rhythm of work, I came back to the goodness of my physical senses, followed by the food, wine and song with the Cretans.

October 31

Awoke to a room of 5 people – it was good. Spent the morning not even attempting to find work, but felt pretty bad about it. Steve consoled me with the fact that the others might be in the same position some day. I was really happy. I felt he was a person one could learn a lot from. Steven and Lennie left me in the afternoon. I washed myself and my clothes and cleaned the room. I went shopping feeling really clean.

Two travellers stayed the night bringing fresh energy. It was a tight space for two more bodies but Steve and his quiet companion were laid-back and easy, and sitting round close together helped us relax. We slipped into a peaceful equanimity, sharing the space in true hippie give and take. Steve sang Donovan songs on his guitar in the candlelight, ouzo was passed around, and our common values prevailed. I was drawn by Steve's lightness and warmth and the next day I felt like travelling away with him, yet something pinned me down in Timbaki.

Later.
Help help help help. What. My head is cracking and feels half blown at the moment. On my own again. Out in the wilderness, yet I'm in a room full of three people. I'm weak when I think its just me. I'm powerful if God is with me, that is if I'm aware of him being there.

The positive atmosphere evaporated once we were back as a foursome the next day. I felt the others resented me for not going to work with them but nothing was said. The lovers were awkward together and the tension increased in the little concrete room. I felt trapped and overwhelmed yet unable to leave. I don't know who I was asking for help from, but I believed that if I could open to something bigger I could find some power – or did I mean peace? Yet I was too caught in my inner struggle to be able to receive. I was knotted up and didn't know how to name what I felt, and no one else spoke about what was happening. I had travelled with Eddie and Pierre since the boat journey to Israel, but sharing that travelling history wasn't what kept me there. I don't know what did. Perhaps some old family dynamic reimposing itself, or simply because I was still hooked on Pierre, idolising him like a dog at his heels.

Tonight is now, writing now. I want to just be and not desire anything else or I'm not free. Ok maybe. But what is this energy? Strong feeling to discover, to get my head together, to create, to be what I am and meant to be. Its desire, and its good.

Later that Halloween night I was with my familiar inner conflict: to be or to do. But I never let go of the importance of the desire to create.

November 1

Working today with Eddie and Beth on the doctor's land. He picked us up from Pavlo's, and we drove to the olive trees. It was a really beautiful place with every kind of fruit tree – oranges, lemons, limes, bananas, blackberries, pomegranates, mandarins, olives and a wild rose tree. The olive work was picking them off the ground into baskets. It was very hard on our backs, and there were armies and armies of mosquitoes. I was pretty well eaten up, and I got really pissed off with them, with olives, with everyone. Every time I killed one I felt torn apart between my conscience and my rational mind. This evening Pierre said if you really come to love them they won't hurt you. I think I believe him, I don't know what I believe in though. I will write to Daddy I think, and ask him.

The mosquitoes were big, and not the odd one or two. The shadows under the trees bristled with anticipation as I entered the orchard. I was in enemy territory, and the merciless squadrons waited in readiness. I was blind to the bald facts: Eddie and Beth were wearing tough jeans and I was wearing my thin, well-travelled hippie skirt, no problem to a mosquito's proboscis. I didn't have a chance in the damp, humid orchard. As the remorselessly slow, hot hours staggered by, my body was offered up to a feeding frenzy. I didn't protest. I believed I was with friends. Eddie and Beth had taken on Pierre's teachings and gave me cool looks when I tried to fend off the insects. Pierre had taken the form of my wise spiritual teacher. How could he be wrong?

A part of me knew his spiritual teachings were off, but that knowing was hidden, curled up tight inside me, and I felt spiritually inferior. I didn't see the cruelty in his admonishing, despite the fact he behaved like a Jain in his extreme aversion to hurting any form of life. There was no give in his rules, no compassion. He was not open to a middle way.

We were all influenced by him, the charismatic French Armenian. But I was in conflict, torn between my own gut feelings and his philosophies that he communicated with elegant surety. I blamed myself for not fully accepting his beliefs. I felt a growing isolation over the weeks as I struggled to adapt myself to his doctrines. I had no inkling I might simply be ok as I was. I was allergic to insect bites, and my legs swelled up in great red welts that threatened to become septic.

November 2

Woke feeling shitty, shitty, shitty. Felt there was an atmosphere of three to one brought about by me. I got up and out of the house as quickly as possible, to buy some food. Came back and the others went to market. Came to a happier state between me and my head by thinking and writing. That's another thing or part of it. I have to have meaning. I have to know the colour of the bones below the flesh. But how astray am I there? Need there be a meaning? Should I simply accept all as it is? I can't yet. I know that so many things have no meaning – the cold at night, the dirt and sordidity [sic] *of this room, when I so believe in purity of spirit – it affects my mind. And the dirt in the minds of the men of the town and in the mind of my assaulter on the beach. Are they all children of God? I feel a bit better now – having gone over things in my head. Oh why do I blow things up to such a degree, it's pointless worrying about the state of my consciousness, and well, my whole self in general. I feel almost criminal in the last few days to be wanting or desiring anything after Pierre's 'lecture.' I get him completely, but for me 'want' still exists because I have to feel a pull or desire for creating something otherwise I would sit and do nothing. I'm so afraid though – everything I say I feel is wrong – am I afraid of the wrath of God?... I seem to have no convictions, no sureness about anything. Maybe things have to be practised and proved before I can believe in them. One thing I am sure about though, is my faith. Its small, but its there.*

My habit of intense inner searching always brought a change of mood. Writing things out in the privacy of my little diary helped me discover what I was feeling, though I was blind to my self-critic.

All three of my friends challenged me about my place at art college, telling me it was an artificial, institutional way of learning, not a genuine way to live.

'It's all on their terms, don't you see Carrie?', said Eddie.

'It's a nine to five existence. Not real life. People teach you art, but it's disconnected from reality. You get there at nine and leave at five. What's real about that?'

Pierre, without turning round from stirring a pot of veg on our little camping stove, observed definitively: 'Eet 'as no value. Zhere is no connection wiz zee earth or wiz zee people. Eet ees in zee head only.'

Listening to them I felt truth in their words. Despite my struggles, I loved the idea of really living close to the earth as Pierre and Beth had done for years. I imagined committing myself to a simple lifestyle and feeling at peace. They inspired me with their experiences. Beth had lived in an isolated village in India for three months, getting to know the people and their culture without seeing one European. Pierre had lived in a similar way in Morocco. They believed the only way was to live connected to the earth – which meant living with people who did that, and to learn by living. Eddie had been to art school but then rejected it, planning to use his art simply as a means to live on. They all put freedom and love above everything else, aiming to rid themselves of the desire for material things.

They also challenged me about my plans to go to a kibbutz. They said I would be enclosed in an international community, and not come into contact with local people or culture.

But in my letter home I had made my mind up:

> *They believe there is much more to learn the way they are doing it, and more learnt compared to my return to an institution with no freedom. I can understand them, yet I feel a need to be taught further by a teacher. I've been swayed but pretty much convinced what I want to do is right for me.*

I am struck by the maturity in my teenage letters. Despite my insecurities, my thinking was clear. Although my emotional self, with its wild eddies and currents, was hidden from my parents, a strong cord of love existed between us.

I enjoyed the discussions with Pierre and Beth. I had never met people who lived like they did. It was exciting to hear their stories about living intimately with people of very different cultures and learning strange languages. Beth described the rituals in India she had witnessed and the customs around birth. She told us about Simmanantannaya in the Hindu religion, the wearing of red or green glass bangles from the seventh month of gestation, how the sound of these bangles is believed to reach the womb and comfort the foetus. To ward off evil, a small dot often in the shape of Om is drawn behind the baby's ear using kohl, a carbon-based make up. I learnt a lot from them, in the way they lived, and in the ideas they brought back.

I was inspired by their passion in living their dreams and I liked our simple life, sharing what we had, and living and working close to the earth. But our differences were a pivot that gradually helped me see what I wanted. I could not commit to my life being forever like this. I wanted to travel further East but I was not prepared to abandon my return.

But nothing stayed static for long. The next day, after failing to find work, Beth and I went to Matala and bumped into Jaco and Migel, her Portuguese friends she knew from India. With no knowledge of where friends were, unlike now with social media tracking every move, meetings were serendipitous and often synchronistic.

Anyone could come along at any time, and it seemed to happen just when you'd be thinking or talking about them. After the joyful meeting we walked to Komo beach and got stoned together, witnessing with enormous pleasure the sun melting slowly into the sea, turning purple, plum and finally grey. In the fading light we walked back to Matala where Blake lived, the friend of Eddie's I'd met on my first night there. I wanted to sleep on his roof again with the starry dome of sky above me, but he was nowhere to be found and I slept in his van.

November 4

> *Had coffee... Nescafe... With Jasmin and Declan in the incredible civilisation of their home. I was surprised to feel at ease with myself. The others arrived; Beth, Pierre, Jaco and Migel and talked about Israel. It may be difficult to get in now because of the profusion of offers of help for the kibbutz. Migel and Jaco were in Israel tripping when the war broke out... Maybe the country has a secret oil supply as there were no restrictions – anyway for cars during the blackout. They are holding a whole Egyptian army surrounded without food or water. Israeli atmosphere is good because of unity among people through war.*

Jasmin and Declan were a couple renting a little cottage up the valley away from Matala beach. I hadn't met them before and I walked into a room flooded with light from their wild and sunny garden. An old olive tree leaned over the door and, as I stood in the doorway, the couple turned to greet me. Usually I felt shy in people's homes for the first time, but these two had an infectious warmth that made me feel at home. Having instant Nescafé was a great luxury. It was my staple drink at home and I missed it. The cafés only sold strong Turkish coffee (renamed Greek coffee after the invasion of Cyprus the following year), which I could only stomach occasionally.

In our little room in Timbaki that evening Eddie offered me keef, but I refused knowing it would confuse my clarity. Pierre, Eddie and Beth were contentedly talking and laughing but I felt an energy pushing me on to Israel and I threw Beth's I Ching for guidance. I got the hexagram "Hsu / Waiting", which told me to; "Wait. Eat, drink and be merry." That stumped me, but the I Ching nearly always gave me a fresh angle on my situation and I let go of my urgency. That evening in the candlelight, I drew some "oms" and yin and yang.

November 5

I met Sashi and Seb and Colin in the Souvlaki cafe pissed out of their heads. Pierre, Eddie and Beth came and then we all found ourselves being driven across Crete in a London taxi to their house in the tiny deserted village of Kalanera.

Seb and Sashi were a Scottish brother and sister who had driven from London in a black cab with their friend Colin. The siblings were beautiful, both with long red hair and wild eyes. They acted like lovers, pronouncing their unerring love for each other across the table that night, downing bottle after bottle of retsina. They laughingly told us about their long and difficult journey from London with its many breakdowns and adventures. Colin was quiet and watchful. I trusted him. As they chattered away, his eyes revealed a silent affection and concern for them. We told them about our ideas for community. How we wanted to find a bigger house and lots of plans. Pierre wanted to build an oven so we could bake bread, Beth wanted us to start a regular practise of yoga and meditation, and Eddie and I wanted to draw and paint. Seb and Sashi told us they had found an amazing deserted village on the edge of a long beach in the Messara bay and urged us to come. Their exuberance was catching and we all seven piled into the taxi. It was dark when we arrived and we slept on the floor of a little house with two rooms with the sound of the waves softly breaking through the night.

November 6

Woke early so managed to jump in the taxi with Dylan singing out loud and a beautiful sun rising. Mist lying shallow in the valley. Somehow the beauty was muted seen through sleepy eyes, made subtle. Worked all day with Eddie for a quiet Greek man who brought us salami and bread. We were bending down weeding around some low growing plants. I was shattered. Felt I must talk to Eddie about things and explain I'm not the bitch I appear to be. But the words refused to come. The communication between us was like dried up mouldy tomato leaves. Felt the separation from the three and my isolation growing every second tonight.

In the morning Seb gave me and Eddie a ride into Timbaki. It was a joy to hear the nasal drawl of Bob Dylan at full volume on the tape recorder, singing out "Sad Eyed Lady of the Lowlands".

But despite the plans for community my relationships were wearing thin, especially with Eddie. The next day I went to Blake's and spoke for hours about my troubles.

'I feel like I'm an outsider, but I don't know what I'm doing that makes them not like me.'

'Carrie you need to relax. It's probably nothing to do with you, you're just taking it on. You're too sensitive, imagining things.'

'I keep leaving the door open and Pierre gets annoyed about that.'

'So what, let him be annoyed, that's his problem.'

Blake was concerned and interested in how I was doing. He was older and a good listener, and I spoke freely about my worries. His firm counsel that I should be more assertive was hard to adopt, but I always felt easier when I left.

It was a still and lovely evening and I met Beth and we walked along Komo beach back to Kalanera, the deserted village. On the way, feeling more confident after my talk with Blake, I decided to tell her about my assault. It felt like a good time to talk.

'Beth,' I began hesitantly, 'you know that day we worked for Antoine in different places and I went off on my own to his polytunnel by the beach?'

'Yeah?'

'Well something happened to me on the beach.'

Beth was gazing out to sea and I went on.

'A guy jumped on me and . . .'

She interrupted: 'What beach, I thought you were working in the polytunnel?'

'I was, but I was on the beach having a break.'

'So what happened?'

'I . . . It was really . . .'

'Yeah I know, those Greek men! Someone came up in the café and stroked my leg before I even saw him!'

'Yes, it's . . . annoying.'

'Drives me crazy. But we're strong women Carrie. What do you mean he jumped on you?'

I suddenly felt unsafe, unable to speak about the shock I'd had. In the face of Beth's assertiveness my words fled. I had lain awake the night after the assault with my body shaking, but now the moment had gone and I didn't tell her. Instead I lifted my chest and shifted focus.

'It doesn't matter. I got rid of him.'

Beth stopped on the sand and turned to me. She had taken in what I was saying.

'What did he do? Were you alone on the beach?'

'Yes, but its ok.'

Her eyes searched my face.

'I remember now, you came back looking wild, strange somehow. So what happened?'

'Oh you know, he tried it on, but I screamed and he ran.'

Beth laughed, as I hoped she would, gave me another quizzical look then turned to walk on. I followed.

'Of course you're ok. You're strong like me.'

She swept her arm across the view, presenting it to me.

'But look we're here,' She exclaimed. 'Let's be here in this beauty!'

Our footsteps crunching in the sand were loud in the silence and my heart felt raw. But walking the miles, because it was so beautiful, the calm sea touched me with its peace. As we drew closer to Kalanera the scent of wood smoke drifted towards us.

November 8

> *Drove again, across the plain, over the hill at six-thirty with Dylan on the tape, in the unreal state of half awakening, watching the sun rise behind us. But it seems a stage has come to an end, no more work for the time being. But today somehow we felt no rush to go back to Kalanera and stayed here in Timbaki. Before the meal Pierre suddenly said he could not eat because of the state of the room for one, and the fact that all the veg should have been prayed over. Eddie who cooked it, had his pride injured, for it was food made with love. None of us could eat. Pierre said it was just his feelings but still, nobody could eat. Knowingly or unknowingly he imposes his ideas very strongly. But basically, he just wanted more meaning put into the grace.*

Back in Timbaki it was a relief that tensions were between the others and nothing to do with me. In the morning I went to Festos, an ancient centre of Minoan civilisation twenty miles from the sea. My lift dropped me at the turning, and I walked up the hill past orange trees and mules. I saw some tourists already there and kept to myself, feeling as usual like a race apart. It was peaceful wandering around the ruins and I relished being alone, meditatively taking in the atmosphere and sketching the ancient frescos. I came to thinking my difficulties were being caused by simply being with people non-stop. It had been ages since I had time out on my own and I sat and gazed out over the mountains of Ida and Asteroussia and across to the bay of Messara.

Sitting there I wrote home:

I am here being blown over by the beauty of Kriti. Its full of the atmosphere of its mystical mythical past

November 11

I understand why Beth said she got so high playing drums. I felt the same thing today.

At Blake's house people were gathering, old friends and new. A man in a loincloth took up a drum and picked out a bare rhythm. People fell quiet, listening as Blake responded to the rhythm on another drum. His hands playfully pattered out a light yet strong and ringing response, dancing around the simple beat of the first drum, whose steady stroke gave anchor to the playfulness. More hands joined in, and soon all our drums fell into a rolling canter, uniting the ambience, conversing with drums not words, the rhythms rising and falling. Sometimes broken-up rills sang out, rising with joyful abandon against the common beat. Out of a group of friends and strangers, the drums unified us deeper than words.

I had got high while chanting on the bow of the ferry to Crete, but in Matala I experienced longer and more consistent states of bliss. The drumming always started spontaneously. Someone would pick up a drum and start a rhythm and others joined if they felt moved. Then a chant would be called out, more often than not a Sanskrit chant from India, and if it gelled, the group would sing with it for hours, building to crescendos and quietening to slowness over and over through the night. At times the drums ceased and then our voices alone sang out through the open windows over the dark beach and across the water. In the candle-lit flickering space, time unravelled and we drummed into the early hours. I let go deeply into other states of being. My mind was empty, I wasn't thinking about what I'd do tomorrow or about the others who sat around me drumming and singing. Nothing else mattered as I entered the sound, following it with my hands and voice, feeling I was one voice rising and falling through the night.

I've never experienced that bliss again while drumming or totally surrendered to the sound and rhythm as I did then. I had absolutely no self-consciousness, blossoming in the freedom of the spiritual atmosphere of the time.

November 12

Woke up. First time I've spent the night in a London taxi – on Kriti! Everyone had hangovers and various non-feelings. I felt happy. Seb lay asleep while everyone made pancakes and attempted to make pancakes, and tidy up. The sun shone outside, on Brad reading at a table in the deserted cafe, on Sammy and Pierre sitting, playing with the sand and talking, and on Eddie and Beth standing way down by the water. I drove with Colin and Seb to Timbaki. Decided to go to the caves in Kamares. We headed up and up into the mountains. No one knew of any caves so we drove down and found an old fortress standing on a hill. The atmosphere was drugged with beauty. It was windy yet still, so full with the voices of long gone days, calling, singing, shouting and eating. Now all asleep. Drove down a path to Timbaki. Such an amazing car ride sliding down winding mud paths. We seemed lost, but Colin drove on though Sashi wanted to turn round. I felt like a happy child. As I return to the earth of my childhood so I return to adventure.

I loved throwing caution to the wind and I loved that part of me. Despite his quiet calm I detected a recklessness in Colin, yet I still trusted him. I have no idea if he knew whether we would come out in Timbaki when we turned down the muddy track. It may have led anywhere, a cliff edge even. In the twilight, the steep, muddy sheep track was hardly wide enough for a car and it felt impossible and crazy. We slid down with little control over the steering, veering from side to side – and I loved it. That impulsiveness, a decision made unanimously by all of us in that moment, gave me a shot of excitement that made me higher than any hashish.

November 13

Went to work with the guy who owns the Creta cinema. Weeding tomato beds again with Beth and Pia and Franz, 2 Austrians staying in the house in Timbaki, It was difficult getting back into work again, but it slowly came together. In the afternoon so many thoughts speeding through my head again, like all the other days working – had the same effect. Contemplated taking a trip – felt I would probably hallucinate up people from home and talk to them. Also came to realisation reason why my mind is confused is because it complicates so much, when reality is just so simple. As the lilies… need nothing, so they also worry about nothing. How near is that cow chewing grass... Or when will the next rain be. They all accept and are now. Everything is simple and beautiful if you look at it that way.

Although working in the fields had been tough to start with I was getting stronger and found it mentally therapeutic. Out on the plain with the distant view of the mountains the repetitive task released a flow of thoughts. It was too hot to chat as we worked up and down along the rows of tomatoes – which was good as my thoughts shifted into a different state, and I had new insights and understandings. The Austrians kept up well but the Cretans were expert, faster than all of us, yet never chided us at our slower pace. The others had been talking about taking acid or peyote. I didn't want to. I had an intuition it would not go well for me. But I felt torn as I wanted to be part of it. The others assured that it was not dangerous as long as it was taken in the right way, but my instinct held me back.

November 14

I had a cold and had decided not to work. Everyone expected me to this morning so I got myself together to go. Am I just being weak and dependent by going along with the sway of Eddie and Pierre, of work and more work, or just lazy not to want to go? I feel a bit of both. After lunch after feeling at the end of all my mental and physical resources I had a burst of renewed energy. Something from somewhere seemed to completely fill me and carry me up, beyond the monotony of work. I felt strong and wise. Maybe it was the fact I would be leaving this scene in the next few days. Billy the American guy came. He is so quiet and beautiful. He travelled on the next day but I think I fell in love with him realising who he was that evening. It hurts to even write about it now. An Irish woman turned up later called Mary with her friend Pete. She got very drunk and everyone found her funny.

This was not the first time I fell in love with someone who would have been kinder to me than Pierre. But I did not follow my heart. Instead Brad, a tall American who had bought a camper van in Chania asked me if I wanted to travel around Crete with him. He was older than me and felt like a big brother. He was straight, not much of a hippy. He told me he had a business in the States that ran itself without him for months at a time so he could go off travelling. It was clear we weren't attracted to each other, but I needed a break and he wanted a companion. More travellers were arriving in Timbaki. Mary and Pete were very confident. They were lively and funny and gathered people round them. But I was ready to leave and see more of the island.

November 16

Told Pierre and Beth this morning I was leaving Timbaki. I should feel free, but somehow it took a lot of courage to actually say the words. I think I've been oppressed by the strength of their personalities. Pierre was amazing. He said, 'Try to be alone'. I will if I can.

Pierre's parting words surprised and touched me. I didn't think he knew how important it was for me to be alone. I went off with Brad the next day, happy to find a travelling companion who gave me security without involvement. We drove East through wild, dry countryside with wild sage, marjoram and thyme coming in warm, scented waves through the windows. My eyes delighted in the new landscape, the ever-present lilac mountains on our left and the sea far down to our right.

I wrote to my parents:

The island is covered in olive trees which are a beautiful grey and the soil is a creamy, grey, clay colour everywhere. Looking down rolling valleys after just climbing a mountain it looks like velvet dotted with green points of embroidery. In the evenings the mountains go purple, yellow and blue in the shadows. The oranges are really ripe now so we are never without vit. C anyway.

We swung through stands of pine and Cyprus searching for a village called Arvi. Once there, we landed in Emmanuel's Café and over coffee met two American sisters Sharon and Cindy. Brad was overjoyed to meet some fellow Americans and became lively and animated. I felt the strong difference in our culture as they chatted away together and I listened quietly.

November 18

I walked down through the village hoping to go to Mass.

The next morning was a Sunday, and I wanted a place of calm after the Americans' fulsome reminiscing about hometowns back in the States. I opened the door to a small church to be welcomed by a serious priest in long black robes. I was hoping to find a beautiful ornate interior like the Greek Orthodox church I'd peeped into in Cyprus. Incense had been pouring out of the door, and the strong haunting tones of the liturgy drew me in, but in Arvi the little church was new and uninspiring and I left.

> *Then coffee at Emmanuels' and a cake. I can't really afford it, but still. I wrote a letter to Tina. It's all incredibly peaceful here, but for some reason my head is not at peace. I realise what a great guy Emmanuel is. I hope I see him again. I'm always afraid to get too near communicating with the Greeks because so many have made me suspicious. Wrote a rather bad intense poem about my head-flipping out over the sunset.*

It was refreshing to meet a Greek man who was genuinely open and friendly. As in Athens, most of the Cretan men regarded us travelling women as sex objects and I approached them warily. A few days previously, alone in our room in Timbaki, a wizened old man tottered in, so small, frail and desiccated he seemed paper thin. We stood facing each other and I smiled and said, 'Kalimera', feeling warmth towards this ancient being who had ventured in to say hello, or so I thought. Suddenly he lurched towards me, his eyes glued on my sex, his hand clutching the air towards it. I was astounded, my concept of the gentle, wise elder obliterated. I shouted, 'Get out, Get OUT of here!', and babbling and shaking he stumbled away. I knew there was no physical danger, I was much the stronger, but I was shaken up, betrayed by my assumption that age has a cut off line for misogyny. Reflecting on his behaviour, in all likelihood he had dementia, an illness I hadn't heard of then.

November 19

> *We woke up to find Cindy and Sharon had gone shopping in Iraklion. Brad freaked a little – she had no shopping list. I made a fairly successful omelette. So satisfying to be cooking here with the sunshine coming down in streaks outside through the bamboo porch. And the only thing disturbing the stillness: a few flies, a bumble bee, distant voices of people working in the fields. What more? Everything here is simple, basic and beautiful.*

The American girls were renting a little house up on the hill and asked us over to eat with them on our second night in Arvi. We feasted on Russian soup, rice, mixed vegetables, fresh bread and peanut butter. The next day they went shopping in Iraklion so we had the house to ourselves. It stood above the village on the hillside, just five minute's walk from the beach. It felt so relaxing for me to be alone there with Brad who was quiet and self-contained. It was a restorative break after the daily search for work and the cramped living quarters in Timbaki.

> *This afternoon I took a chair and put it outside the room*

facing the sunset and meditated. Realised it doesn't matter what position you are in if it feels 'endaxi'. I always know when it's good as I come away with such a sense of total peace and calm. Tonight a voice came in stronger than usual – a few short sentences with pauses. I can only remember a few. 'Absorb this stillness, be, with the peace, be at one with the surroundings. Absorb, absorb.'

The form of my spiritual practice wasn't important, but how I felt inside was. It didn't matter to me whether I was in a mosque, a church or under the sky, as long as it felt ok, or endaxi. I had sensed an inner voice before, but this time it had a calm, clear authority. I sat in the peaceful evening air in a state of connection and wholeness. Living in or close to nature, cooking, eating, sleeping and washing, I felt more alive and at peace. Living close to her skin, the earth helped me be more aligned with myself, and meditating in the open air gave me clearer insights.

I was reading "The Centre of the Cyclone" by John Lilly, which I'd picked up from a table in a café in Timbaki, fascinated by the title that hinted at an eternal place inside the storm of the ego. The woman it belonged to saw me engrossed and handed it to me with a smile. Something about his description of a workshop he ran in 1971 in Esalen, the epicentre of the human potential movement in the States, moved me. He had given a few simple words to the participants to repeat, a statement affirming a deepening with mother. I felt them as a fusing with mother earth. As I sat quietly, his words resonated inside me and

I felt the intimate presence of the earth all around. It was definitely a her and she felt like a conscious being, one I could unite with. I had a sense of a nurturing mother. I was in touch with the zeitgeist of the time, as unbeknownst to me, as yet unpublished, James Lovelock was defining the Gaia hypothesis, which identified the earth as one whole interconnecting organism.

John Lilly was a scientist and mystic who passionately explored altered states of consciousness and researched and experimented with LSD in flotation tanks to expand his spiritual experience. He worked with Fritz Perls who developed Gestalt Therapy, and Ida Rolf the creator of Rolfing, to release trapped emotions in his body. His book was revolutionary for me. It was the first time I had heard of body-based therapies, and putting spiritual practice together with that kind of personal growth work was radical, and still is. Ram Dass had identified for the West the spiritual practice of being present in his seminal counter-cultural bible "Be Here Now". I was having lessons from nature of being in the moment, as nature is eternally present and cannot be otherwise. Like Lilly, Ram Dass also explored psychedelic drugs along with Timothy Leary and others, rejecting them when he realised the sublime states he reached always disappeared when the drugs wore off. As I learnt from reading "Be Here Now" in Athens, Ram Dass found his teacher Maharajji and a slower, harder, but more long lasting approach to self-realisation.

The people don't reflect the simplicity. Walked into town

feeling shitty. Couldn't face talking to the French guy. Walked off and had a tsai with the family at the cafe eating their lunch. Walked back along the beach to Brad. Sunbathed a little more. Went up to the house.

My meditation that afternoon had been profound, but interactions with people afterwards brought me down and my serenity vanished. I blamed people for disrupting my high and was grumpy. I had no idea of the next step: of bringing my awareness from meditation into relationships and that life itself could be a practice. I didn't yet know that was the real work of spiritual growth.

I had no shoes

November 20

Next day I climbed up a hill in the early morning to watch the sunrise purposing to meditate again. The sun was just out of the water but very beautiful. I had little result meditating: maybe it was because I had planned to do it the night before and so it was forced. Or maybe because I missed the initial sun rise... I picked some red heather and a few doves circled above me. It was cold with the faint warmth of the early sleepy sun. Left Arvi midday. Good to be moving again. Brad drove slowly into Ierepetra and I began to write a letter home. French Louis came up to me much happier than when we met in Timbaki when he had rather an untogether head... It was good to see him and he was much happier – working on a construction site for 200 dracs a day. The difference between him and Brad came over very strongly and who I related to more. Louis was a brother; gave me his sandals. I had them tightened at a shoe menders. They are strong and fit me well. He had no money when he travelled to here from Matala and was given food, dope and a place to stay every night. Why do I worry?

At this point I was without shoes. I had been limping from my infected bites, unable to walk properly, which caused my cheap Greek sandals to break. Despite the poor state of my feet, living without any footwear was freeing. I liked the feeling of my soles thickening and growing more animal-like. I trusted something would turn up and it did. Louis was a free spirit, happy to be with or without money and possessions. He had an open heart and I felt touched by his fluidity and freedom. In comparison, Brad seemed overly serious and practical. I may have been free from attachment to material possessions but I was also cut off from my body. I had been ignoring the infections in my legs and they were worsening.

November 21

I made breakfast of fried eggs and greeted the various Greeks passing by on their donkeys. Then driving inland to Sitia. I hobbled around as my foot is now infected too, bought some cream for it. We reached Mohlos – tiny village by the sea with an ancient church across on island opposite. A poor old Greek lady gave me some bread and fish and oranges. I sit in her one-room house and contemplate; the poorer they are the more they give. And I sit there from a home with 14 rooms and all I could give her was box of matches.

I had wondered off through a tired and overgrown olive grove and a tiny, wizened old woman came up to me. She invited me into her one-room little house. She lived in total poverty: just a dirt floor and the absolute basics for life. She gave me a piece of hard bread and some very dried-up fish. I held it in my hand repulsed, but looking down at her dark, brown wrinkled face looking up at me I couldn't refuse and swallowed it down. From my appearance, she may have thought I was as poor as her. The least I could do was accept her hospitality.

She was the poorest person I had met and the most generous. The comfortable spacious home I came from made me feel ashamed at the little I had to give. Unlike her, I was choosing to experience life very simply. Her one room house was zen-like in its bareness. I looked into the dark interior and she gestured to me to enter. In the corner sat her husband, bent over, small and wrinkled, an almost exact replica of her. He didn't raise his head. There was a low bed against one wall, a small table and chair, and a shelf with some other small scraps of food sitting on it. My host put a filthy bowl on the side and filled it with scraps of grey morsels. I waited nervously, thinking it was intended for me, but she took them outside. I followed her round behind the hut to find a little enclosure fencing in one old, scrawny goat. Their life was so meagre and I let it all in. Suddenly their reality overwhelmed me and I had to leave. As I said goodbye she held my gaze, her eyes fearlessly penetrating mine. What I saw in them was strength.

I was jolted by this old couple's reality. They teetered on the edge of survival and it scared me. Their poverty was real whereas mine was an experiment. I had the backing of a secure and comfortable home, however simply I chose to live. But for me to grow I had to leave my comforts behind and explore the world. I wanted no possessions to hide behind. That freedom enabled the trust and equality with fellow travellers on the road, even if our lives were very different back home. This was the refreshing change I was loving, so different from my upbringing where money separated me from those without it.

Having so few belongings meant I had a vital relationship to those I did have. I loved the things I carried in my small rucksack and my little diary was always at hand.

Now I have so much accumulated stuff I forget what lies at the back of my cupboards. Being unattached to possessions was an ability Izzy continued to have all her life. Years later I was shocked when she told me she hadn't paid the rent on her storage after she moved, and all her possessions were requisitioned to pay off the debt. But after listening to me, she said peacefully, 'You know, I feel freer now, losing all that stuff. They were just things after all.'

22 November

Left for Iraklion after porridge. It was so hot and good it seems to bring me back to home civilisation again. I found a shop and bought antibiotics for my foot and swollen throat and glands. 6 dracs for each pill. A rip off. Bought brown bread and yoghurt. Sitting in the van later, Colin and Sashi appeared with an incredible story to tell. Mary and Pete were in jail. Mary had bought a car for £20.00 in a 2 minute decision. Then she got pissed in Antonios while Pete was flirting with a German girl. He went over the road to a hotel and she went to look for him. He emerged completely disrobed and they drove off together, Mary driving. But at the first bend she crashed right into the military camp. They threatened to shoot them after pulling them out of the car. They spent the night in Timbaki cell with hands and feet tied together. Transferred to Iraklion. Mary was done for no driving licence and biting an officer…

We were all wild and free on Crete, and the Cretans allowed us our freedom. But Mary and Pete were even wilder, stretching freedom to an extreme, pushing the boundaries out so far they crashed back on them with the full force of the Cretan Military. Feeling sorry for them Brad and I went to the jail and took them books and oranges. They were very muted. That evening Colin and Sashi went to see them too and joined us for a meal in the van, bringing retsina, yoghurt and halva.

November 23

Went to the prison again and said goodbye to Mary and Pete. They seemed even more subdued having had no fresh air or sunshine. It was sad leaving them. We picked up about 10 people after having a shower in the YHA. Drove to Knossos and walked round the incredible ruins of King Minos's palace. On again to Hania. Everybody invaded an interesting little crash pad named 49. I suddenly met lots of really friendly people and a Canadian guy who seemed slightly different who I could relate to more. He is a good person. But I hate having to say goodbyes. It will crack me a little this time. Love is the wrong word, anyway its unexplainable, but I feel too much for people sometimes.

I was experiencing my responses to a range of humanity I had never met in the seclusion of the English countryside. I fell in love in seconds and grieved the parting for hours. Brad was steady as a rock, impassive and generous, ignoring my emotional turbulence and packing as many people into his van as he could as we drove along. I gave no further thought to the couple in prison. They thought they would be let out soon and we had done what we could.

November 24

Happy morning. Stepped out of the van into sunshine and Hania harbour by 49. Bought a bottle of fresh milk and ate brown bread and jam. Went along to the morning scene in 49. Began to make my mark on the wall there. We left with

Mac the beard and Ron and Suzi. Arrived at gateway to the Samaria Gorge with its 10 commandments – for the benefit of tourists… and made a great salad, the best yet. Having 4 people in the van for some reason, seemed incredibly funny, partly because I was stoned. I began to write a really crazy letter to Lotti in that state. It was very cold, the coldest I've been.

The hippie inn in Hania had a large hall covered with travellers' artwork. There was a continuous group of people there drawing and painting. I spent a happy hour sitting on the floor painting a large oak tree, drawing its roots so they wound around other people's drawings and making faces in its leaves. I was sad to leave it unfinished. That night we parked at the top of the Samaria gorge. The other five made sleeping spaces for themselves on the wooden part of the van floor or on their sleeping mats. I was in my thin down sleeping bag, now very worn, and the only space left was the metal floor over the engine. It conducted the cold mountain air outside directly into my body. The top of the Samaria Gorge is high and the temperatures, already falling at sea levels, were icy that night. The pain of the cold cut sharply into my body through the sleepless hours as I turned around and around, trying every position possible, but only succeeding in making all of me more freezing. I would have been better to get out and walk about but I chose to endure. Like any intense pain, it focussed all my attention during that long night.

November 25

Set off for the grand hike down the Gorge after hot porridge with raisins, wheatgerm, cinnamon, sugar and milk. It was a beautiful morning growing slowly warmer as we went further down. I got deafer and deafer, but more and more into it all. Ron, Suzi and Brad sped ahead mostly. I felt it was such a waste to walk fast. There was an endless wave of low humming coming from the wind thro' the trees and a strange echoing flap of a bird's wing. It was strange and different. So much space. So much peace. Wrote 2 lines of poetry and drew a little. Arrived at Samaria, deserted village at the bottom. Running water and wooden table and benches lying on the grass in the sunlight – waiting for us to eat. Brown bread with sardines and feta. Felt such good vibes from that village – completely empty and desolate. Unusual. I felt so happy there. My mind filled up with lots of ideas of spending next winter there. Walking back wasn't so easy. Meant to be the largest gorge in Europe.

My strong body felt no aftermath of the cold as we walked down the gorge, other than having blocked ears from the altitude. I lingered behind the others absorbing everything in the surroundings. I always saw more in a landscape when alone. The atmosphere in the gorge was powerful and still. Ruins had merged with nature and the little village at the bottom of the gorge was enchanting. The others had gone off to explore another path and I was alone.

Seven little stone houses sat around a spring that bubbled

out of the rock before meandering down to join the bigger stream down the gorge. Doors stood open and I wandered around, looking inside dark interiors that welcomed me in. The grass was cropped short, unusually green, being fed from the pure water source. As I knelt down to drink the water welling up between two rocks, a rustling in the shadows made me look up and a Kri-Kri, a large male Cretan goat with his exotic curving horns, stared severely at me just a few feet away. Then he leapt away silently. The place felt at one with its environment, quietly holding memories, though not all happy ones as the last inhabitants were evicted ten years earlier to make the gorge a National Park and to protect the rare Kri-Kri. I fantasised returning there to live with Izzy and some friends and making a community in that magical place. It remained a fantasy.

November 26

> *Today we were two again and drove back to Timbaki. A letter from the kibbutz saying I can come. We drove to Petrokefali and found Kosse and the schoolhouse. A somewhat negative feeling especially with Pierre. Dick and Anita were there. The kitchen is perfect but the other room is too big and cold. Beth took me for a walk and told me more fully what I knew before.*

The journey with Brad had given me much contemplative time to be with John Lilly's book. I was enjoying it and felt, as I had on Ios reading Carlos Castaneda, that my inner journey was aligned to an outer one. Lilly clarified that ego took away so much of what I was searching for: love, joy and conscious awareness. We had driven around the island with all the windows down and I imagined my ego being blown away by the wind.

Pierre, Eddie and Beth had found somewhere new to live but when we arrived Pierre was unfriendly and ignored me. Beth explained he didn't want me to stay. She was concerned about how I felt, but I wasn't rejected. I felt freed up by my trip and from new landscapes and people. Other people were staying in the old schoolhouse as well, and Beth was friendly and I stayed the night there anyway.

November 27

> *Dick expressed his insecurity with me most of the early hours of the morning. It didn't really irritate me, but apparently he has been hassling many other chicks. I still feel there's a reason behind it, he's basically genuine, open and friendly, but not very strong. I split about one, feeling really good vibes towards and from Beth (anyway). Too late to reach Kalanera. I went to Matala. Walked nearly all the way. Went to see Declan and Jasmin. Really established good feelings. I'm so glad. They are very special people. Ate with them and Nico. Saw and added to, their incredible work. Theres a power to their communal drawings thats very dynamic and new. Almost like a new movement moving away from the egotistical big artist figure to a shared art – giving more than one energy – more ideas – more movement.*

I spent the night fending off amorous advances from Dick, a very young and lost traveller that I felt big-sisterly towards. I left for Matala to see Jasmin and Declan again. When I arrived I found them deeply involved in a big artwork. They had their backs to me, sitting cross-legged on the floor and leaning over a low wide table. Once again my beliefs were turned on their heads. Beth and Pierre had already told me art college was an unreal learning environment. Here, even art-making as an individual pursuit was questionable. I gazed at a huge drawing laid across the table next to an altar with candles burning. There was so much to take in. Planets, stars and moons sailed around a matrix of animals and human figures. Their communal work challenged the individual status quo – and it was stunning. All the detail was painstakingly beautiful and seemed to express the harmony that clearly reigned between them as a couple.

I stood by the table and Jasmin offered me a crayon.

'Carrie come and join us. We'll breathe together. Close your eyes and tune in.'

I sat on the floor feeling I was being invited into a kind of ceremony that involved the drawing. I hadn't ever thought of bringing the sacred into art before. I was fascinated, and I loved being summoned to quietness like this.

Beside me, Jasmin took a breath.

'When you feel ready, open your eyes and take in the world in front of you. Let it all in. Become part of it. Then take your crayon and see where it wants to go. What mark it wants to make. We want you to add your energy to the dance.'

Feeling stilled, I opened my eyes and took in the whole scene. I was pulled to a group of female figures dancing in a circle holding hands. They had red and purple dresses swirling around them. In the centre of their circle I reached in and drew a curling green frond emerging from the ground turning its face upwards. The candles flickered and time passed. Above the circle I drew a crescent moon. I heard Jasmin and Declan get up and someone else sat down beside me and I glanced sideways. It was a man I didn't know. He quietly added his creative markings without looking at me. We didn't speak. I felt we were communicating in our shared expression. There was no need for words. I went on till I felt complete and then got up to leave. Declan and Jasmin looked at me and smiled. They didn't look at what I had done, yet I felt acknowledged and included in their collective creation.

> *I walked down to Blake's house feeling inspired. He was clear eyed and happy having found a new woman called Varena. Very together – looks as if it is making him whole. Eddie was there and seemed to be very confused, weird vibrations coming across. Seems to be in some kind of conflict about what kind of attitude to take towards me.*

The next day I met Beth in Timbaki in the familiar little room. We were moving out for good. We took down our home-made shelves and swept the floor. I was happy to walk out and close the door on it. Eddie and Pierre had gone to Iraklion to score, and by late afternoon Beth and I headed out of the town towards Kalanera, in the direction we thought we had driven in the taxi. We found ourselves on a rough track dropping down into an olive grove and followed the winding track through the trees for over an hour as the grove thickened and stretched away in front of us into what was now a forest of olive trees. The light was fading and under the trees it was nearly dark. Soft rain was falling and Beth was jumpy, fearful we were lost. As we walked side by side through the silent wood I reassured her. I had no reason to be confident, yet irrationally I felt sure and happy, and I persuaded her to go on rather than turn back.

There was something about the not knowing on that night walk that I loved. I've always felt called to go outside at twilight. If I were alone in the darkness of that unknown wood I would have been afraid, but with the two of us I felt secure and alive, relishing the soft damp air and felt I could walk for miles in the darkness.

Finally, the faint sound of sea breaking on shingle came to our ears and we glimpsed a light. We felt our way towards it, making out a few low buildings. Yellow light suddenly poured out of an open doorway and singing and laughing fell into the night. We looked in, blinking in the candle light to see Seb and Sashi holding court standing on the two beds, playing guitar and singing while Colin stood stirring a steaming pot of vegetables on a camping stove. They welcomed us in and told us Mary and Pete had been released and were back in Timbaki. Soon we were a warm part of the merriment and the food.

In the morning I went out to explore the deserted village properly for the first time. All the little white houses were sitting in the sand. Everything green had been covered over. I wondered why the villagers had left, but it was probably because of sand migrating up from the beach. They were all small, low, white traditional dwellings, all blending into the blond sand. I walked down to the smallest house that faced the sea and fell in love with it. It was one single room with a tiny fireplace and a chimney, about ten feet square with thick walls and a seaward window. There was a wooden shutter and a wooden door and the floor was covered in sand. I loved its simplicity. It was perfectly clean and peaceful, and I decided to make it my own.

I went back and told the others and picked up my rucksack. No one said much and I returned to my little house, walking in with a sigh of happiness, closing the door behind me. I unrolled my sleeping bag, pushed candles into the sand and lit one to celebrate the occasion, and then arranged my small collection of possessions, my shells, sketchbook and few clothes. I made a fire with some wood I'd collected and felt safe and happy. The house fitted me exactly. It seemed to be made for my proportions. After sharing a room in Timbaki with Pierre, Eddie and Beth and staying in Sashi and Seb's house, it was a welcome change to be with myself alone in my own space.

Kalanera

Cream shadows
In my square room

All around
is wind scream
and sea roar

Inside
it's still

But the brick
fell, shutter slammed
open, lights went out.

My room became the night of howling waves

I closed the shutter,
Lit the candles,
And wrote.

November 29

Found work in Timbaki. Mike, a new inhabitant of Kalanera came along too. Such an incredibly high morning. I was so happy again feeling like I was beginning to talk from my old self again. Still a little rubbish to get scraped out. Work went by forgotten, but getting done. Walked home along the beach. Stopped to finish our meal, bread and fish as the sun set. It was cold and blowing hard and something in me said it was crazy, yet loving it. Going back to that love of falling into things blindfold, jumping into life, that now I realise is so important. A long walk along the dark sand, with a thin sliver of a moon lighting up the rollers.

Mike had appeared by way of the talking grapevine in Timbaki, and moved into an empty house opposite mine. Early in the morning I was sitting in my doorway and he came across and chatted. He told me about his journey from South Africa and his feelings about being a traveller, and how lonely he felt at times. I watched him drawing lines in the sand with a stick, his long black wavy hair blowing across his face, and my body melted in the soft tones of his voice. All day I felt high as we worked together picking tomatoes, culminating in an ecstatic walk back along the beach. That night we curled up together on a narrow single bed in his house. I felt a tender intimacy in our stillness. But it was not to last.

November 30

Lifted myself out of bed with some energy coming from somewhere. Colin drove us in. Started work. Still seems a certain good communication between Mike and I, but he seemed to be in a very negative mood when we stopped work at 12. He is in love with someone at home. It all hit hard today. I felt he took a pessimistic attitude towards me and what I'm trying to do. Told me to go home. True, more courage is taken in going home, but I can build up that courage more by staying where I am. My own feelings are never strong enough when I hold any admiration for the person I'm with. Yet somehow for the first time I felt I was doing right in staying travelling. In ways he is very fucked, as is the way of having such a sensitivity to life. Said rels always very superficial when travelling because of no commitment. So true. But I'm beginning to feel if you are true completely it doesn't matter about no commitment (?) Had he felt that after the previous night? I wish I knew. Felt a gap growing between us because of the difference in opinion. Felt down for the first time in a long time. Such a crash down after having a letter from Izzy.

After opening his heart to me Mike became surly and critical and I was hurt. I retreated to my own space, shut my door, lit a fire and felt protected from the weather – that was now getting colder and rainier. I was soothed by the peace and calm my own little house gave me. It gave me time to return to my heart. I could write and draw away from boisterous Sashi and Seb who were loud talkers and noisy. Although there if I wanted company.

I picked up a letter from Izzy in Timbaki Poste Restante, who wrote to say she had met an Italian man called Angelo and they were living in a cave in the mountains above Matala. She seemed to be going her own way and didn't want to come to Israel. But it was a relief to hear from her and I decided to go and find her in the morning.

December 2

> *I hate to have to admit it but today was very, very negative. I came up to Seb's house to find everyone was tripping. Pierre and Eddie and the others had taken Peyote. This feeling of isolation came over me. As soon as I feel like that I begin to close myself in even more. I can't understand why they didn't ask me if I wanted to. I feel Pierre's attitude towards me influences the others whether they are aware of it or not. He ignored me again almost totally. I feel such a lot for him.*

The step of moving into my own house in Kalanera created a gap between me and the loose-knit community of Eddie, Pierre and Beth who had moved into a larger house with Sashi and Seb. Brad was friendly and parked nearby but that day the feeling of being excluded was intense. Everyone was in a unified drugged trance except for me. There was a strange silence. Pierre stared at me blankly and Colin sat transfixed looking out to sea. I didn't know what to do with myself and felt strange being around them.

My devotion to Pierre made no sense. He was unfriendly and rejecting, yet I continued being infatuated. The attraction I had for him cancelled out all of my self-respect. My feeling for him stayed constant. Something was at stake. I could not bring myself to accept it was going nowhere and I kept hoping. The experience of falling in love with him so deeply in Cyprus had been extraordinary and transformational, and because I had never felt anything like that before, I was hooked on him.

That morning I had been to Matala and found Izzy, but she was focussed on her Italian boyfriend and living in a cave community with a group of people I didn't relate to. I wanted some one-to-one time with her but it didn't happen. Izzy had found her own little community living wild in nature but we seemed to be moving in different directions. I needed her support and wasn't ready to lose contact. But I didn't tell her, I didn't know how. Independence and doing our own thing was our pattern.

December 3

What irrelevant shit I write down. Can't I be content with a few words capturing simply the essence of each day? Yesterday my head was so confused because I felt so rejected – which was such a selfish attitude to take anyway. But I still can't see that clearly yet, partly because of the realisation that basically I do need people. Worked for Manoli today. Walked all the way in, arrived shattered. But maybe up on Mt Ider someone took pity on me. Manoli gave me his motorbike to drive home with.

Being entrusted with a big motorbike was a joy. I loved the autonomy it gave me, and the connection with space and fresh air around my body. I felt safe and free. I knew bikes as I had a smaller motorbike at home. Manoli was not worried about regulations and no papers were exchanged, simply trust. I imagined Zeus, whose home was above me on Mount Ider, bestowing kindness down on me.

December 4

> *Drove into work on the bike early. It was invigorating. So beautiful in the morning with the cold sweet freshness of a new day rushing past your little still self roaring along. Had a cafe, but became a little paranoid by all the police, so walked to the field from Timbaki. Manoli joined me later with hot meatballs, bread, Retsina and some Lebanese… It was very difficult getting back to work again.*

To be astride the big old bike thudding through the warm, dry empty countryside was heaven. I breathed in the wild thyme-scented air, my long hair flying around my unhelmeted face, and felt free. I took off from my new home in Kalanera and had a wonderful ride into Timbaki through the olive groves. Riding the bike felt like a herald of change, proclaiming the imminence of departure from Crete. In Timbaki I got nervous, not because of riding the bike, but because we had heard it was now illegal to work as incomers. There was clearly anger about travellers taking work. Yet I felt impervious of any responsibility and carried on. Despite my near rape experience, I didn't question my actions. I felt supported by Manoli who was down to earth and trusting and wanted nothing more than friendship.

To my parents I wrote:

The majority of the Greeks simply annoy and hassle us females the whole time, but we have made about 2 or 3 genuine Greek friends who make up for the whole lot.

December 5

Beautiful day. Walked into Kamilare and did some shopping. Met Colin, the more I know of the more I get to like. Came back. Mike came and played guitar on the step outside my house – with the sunset. Thats what it needs to lose the empty house feeling – a soaking of songs and voices and people spending time in and around it. It needs infiltrating with 'humanity.' Made some tea – felt so satisfied, having found wood, made a fire, found an old pot and cups, bought the tea – so many simple things but put together create an amazing cup of tea… and such a warmth of satisfaction. Felt a little afraid tonight. It only takes a little imagination to blow that up.

Our tiny village was abandoned and no one asked for any rent. It was on its own, several miles away from any shops or houses. After the first few days of solitary bliss in my new home, the weather was less friendly, becoming windy and cold. In the dark I lay and listened to the waves roaring up the beach towards me a hundred yards away in the dark and felt scared. I knew rationally they couldn't reach me, that there were no tides, but the wind had increased and they were growling with a deeper roar as they flung themselves further up the beach. It was December, the weather was changing, and the sea was now too cold to swim.

December 6

> *Did quite a lot of painting and penwork. Felt stronger today. Collected some wood. Pierre came this evening. Seemed to ignore me a little less. I ate with them – brought down some fish and bread. Partly because he was feeling ill Seb made it obvious how he felt about my presence. It all seems very unreasonable. I can't think what I've done. Richard said the next day you can only get on with so many people. Maybe I try too hard to get on with too many people. But its hard when you have a need to be accepted by everyone.*

Late the previous evening Seb lay on his bed drunk, guitar on his stomach, singing a loud and slurred repetitive song.

"My woman won't fuck me, my woman won't fuck me,
I want her – but my woman won't fuck me."

In my diary I made light of the anguish I felt that night. I walked into the room and was horrified to realise his 'song' was about me. Beth, Pierre, Colin, Brad and Richard, a new arrival, all stood nearby and I froze, my skin burning with shame. I was sure they all knew I was the woman. No one said anything or looked at me. I had ignored Seb's advances as I wasn't attracted to him. The idea of being in bed with him in a room with his sister and Colin was impossible to imagine. I don't know whether he knew in his drunken state he was shaming me. Afterwards he ignored me.

I fell back on my creative resource which as always helped me feel stronger. I drew a serene swan-like image in my little house and was calmed.

December 7

Walked into Timbaki and lifts some of the way. Went to the Poste Restante. The money from M had come through. It gave me such a sense of security – good or bad, but it felt really good. I think basically I must realise I don't really relate to anyone here in Kalimaki, or they don't relate to me, so why keep pushing it, trying to get through to them, trying to find points in common, Decided to leave tomorrow for Israel. Colin and Sashi came up for tea. I like Sashi, but we have practically nothing in common.

It was now possible to get into Israel. When I was travelling with Brad I had used up my hard-earned cash very quickly on fuel, camping gas and food. I asked my mother to send me £16.00, which was the fare for the flight to Tel Aviv from Athens.

Before I left England at the end of August I had worked all summer as a chambermaid at the Bolt Head Hotel in Salcombe in Devon. I was renowned for working barefoot, and I earned sixty pounds. I lived on this for eight months. I had earned my keep on Crete working in the fields but flying out of Greece would take more than I could earn.

December 8

Mike and I made our way to Iraklion ending up in taking the bus. He felt ill and stayed by the port all afternoon. I walked round town feeling not exactly full of energy. It must be the psychological effect of travelling on my ears. Went to the museum – saw the original frescos from Knossos. Really annoys me how they mess around reproducing it all so much. Sat in the gardens and felt very peaceful. Caught the boat at 6.30pm. Beginning to be able to ignore the Greeks curious eyes almost completely now. Arrived Athens about 8.00. Made our way to "Outside Inn." It was strange there, very quiet, very few people.

I had gone to Crete because I couldn't enter Israel, but the seven weeks were an experience that stretched my parameters, triggered emotional tumult, and threw me into chaos. I also landed squarely in my instincts; gritty encounters instigated a pluckiness I'd never needed before in my cosseted childhood – that would last me for life.

6

The Maternal Line

December 9

Last night I dreamt very vividly about Grandmummy – a tiny talkative wispy haired shadow. We drove off in a bus with her next to the drivers seat, turning round all the time making bright conversation. Suddenly she called out enthusiastically, 'We're going to the Promised Land!'

I was waiting in Athens for the plane to Tel Aviv when I had this dream. I had slept in my habitual star-shod bedroom, high up on the roof of the Outside Inn. I was alone there as the inn was almost empty. Now dawn was opening the sky with pink as the city noises drifted up. I lay in my sleeping bag eyes closed, oblivious to all sights and sounds, captivated instead by the faint but unmistakable presence of Miriam my grandmother. We hadn't been close, and she had died suddenly when I was seven. But despite her strictness and formality, the bond had been there and I felt it now.

Filled with this unexpected visitation I lay in the first warm sunbeams and thought back to a conversation with my mother in the summer before I left England.

We were standing by the open French windows and the sun glittered off the sea behind us as we talked about my impending trip to Israel. Looking out at the horizon she said carelessly:

'Miriam was Jewish after all.'

'What do you mean she was Jewish? I didn't know that.'

'Well we never had much to do with that side of the family.'

Amazed, I stared at her, but she turned and walked away. The door had closed, and I knew if I wanted more I would have to wait. I stood trying to grasp the news of my lineage, and felt tricked somehow. Why had she not told me before? I had always thought of my blood from her side being uncomplicated, solidly English. Yet despite my surprise, something was added in that moment. I felt an exotic shadow flickering inside, a little flurry in my soul. I held my head up higher, feeling I was reclaiming something.

Later when darkness fell and we had eaten, my mother said,

'I did see her people a few times, but only at night. It was always long and dark, the journey to Golders Green.'

My ears pricked up and I prompted her.

'Golders Green? That's where they lived?'

'Yes. Mum only took me when he was away. I had to go up to my room and nanny would get me ready while Thomas brought the Bentley round. Mum never went out alone at night so this was very odd, and that I was to come with her. The first time we went she was nervous and wouldn't say anything to me in the car about where we were going. She just talked about my governess.'

'So your father didn't know?'

'I don't know if she told him. Perhaps not.'

There was a pause as we both took this in.

Then I continued: 'Miriam's family name was Sapir wasn't it?'

'Yes. Her mother was Hannah. She was fierce, a big

woman and strong. Miriam had to really hold her own to break away, but then she was strong too. She charmed all the men, especially Howard her father-in-law, your great-grandfather. She could twist him round her little finger. Lucky that she could, as the sisters were not nice to her.'

'You mean your father's eight sisters?'

'Yes, your great-aunts.'

'What were their names again?'

I loved hearing the ring of all the great-aunts' names, emanating from such a different era:

'Beatrice, Eva, Charlotte, Ruby, Gertrude, Violet, Henrietta and Maude.'

'Did she manage to befriend them in the end?'

'I think not. When I was quite young Aunt Violet shocked me by saying, "You don't mind being half-caste then?" I don't think she ever forgave Miriam for marrying their one and only beloved brother.'

I wanted to know more about Miriam.

'She was brave to go off alone – and then marry out.'

'Yes, I think it was unusual. But as you know she got a job as James's secretary and they fell in love. She loved life with him. She was really bright, could have done so much more. He wouldn't let her learn to drive you know.'

'That's incredible to think she was controlled like that, when she was so assertive in other ways. Did she stay in touch with her family?'

'They didn't come to the wedding. It was in a registry office – all very beautifully done of course, with lunch at the Savoy.'

My mother had talked freely, so it seemed, about her mother's family, yet I was left with an aura of unspoken feeling. Years later in 2006, I asked her again. We were disembarking from a plane in Sweden as we travelled to my nephew's wedding. The conversation had come around again to family and relatives and I still felt angry with her because of what I thought was her snobbery, looking down on her poorer, less classy Jewish relatives, how she never included them. We were in the line waiting for passport control. I had asked this question many times, but this time I showed my anger.

'Why didn't you tell me Miriam was Jewish? Why do you dislike that side of the family so much?'

She turned and looked me straight in the eyes.

'Because I was frightened.'

'Oh . . . Mum!'

I was thrown by her admission and felt guilty for pestering her. Fear was a word she never used, but then it dawned on me: it would have been very scary to be a young girl in an anti-semitic London. My mother always seemed indomitable. I had never imagined her silence came from fear. Everything fell into place as I remembered another story. One day as a young woman in 1944 she got into a carriage at Paddington. As soon as she sat down a man leaned his face towards her and said leeringly,

'You're a little Jewish girl aren't you?

She froze in her seat staring at him, then jumped out of the carriage and ran and ran.

Her father's family was solidly English, with an ancient family line she had traced back to the twelfth century. He was much talked about. I knew he was a colonel in the army and was awarded the DSO after the First World War. Being the only brother of eight sisters, he inherited everything, including his duty to support any unmarried sisters for life.

Miriam's sudden death when I was little left me growing up surrounded by her dark antiques, my grandfather's medals, and her exquisitely graded pearl necklace – given to me when I was 18. My mother kept everything, her grief held in the small hard stones that sparkled on her hand each Christmas.

The shock of Miriam's fall, the missed footstep at the top of the stairs, left my mother retelling the story of the accident to me for years. The terrible journey to London, meeting the two uncles on the steps of the morgue – who fled when her back was turned, abandoning her to identify her mother's body alone. Then the lonely journey home with the stop in the pub when she could drive no further, sitting head in hands, attracting strange looks.

Years later I looked up my Jewish relatives. A second cousin, a funny vivacious woman, told me Miriam was an expert seamstress and made exquisite smocked dresses for her nieces that she sent in the post every Christmas. She said Miriam's brother was very close to her and he longed to meet his niece, my mother. He came to visit after Miriam died, but my mother was out.

For me in 1973, hearing I had Jewish blood before I left home felt like discovering an exciting forgotten drawer in my history. My dream ignited a connection to Miriam and my newly discovered lineage. I was more than ready now to get to "The Promised Land". After three months of diversions, I was truly on my way.

December 11

> *On the plane I felt really confident. The first flight I have enjoyed. Arrived Tel Aviv about 10.00pm. The whole place hit me really pleasantly. Crashed in the airport on the floor under a window. Slept deep. In the morning left Mike rather abruptly in the bus station. Caught a bus to a junction near the kibbutz, not knowing where it was. Met a little Israeli soldier who hitched with me to the drive. First impressions: I don't usually have any anyway – my mind simply absorbs, becomes a valve letting it all go through without a comment or reaction.*

I remember a strange sensation in my chest when I woke up in the airport. As I looked out of the window I felt something open and broaden around my heart. There was an ancient quality in the slow curve of the horizon, with its tawny browns and golds that spread out on all sides. It called me with a strange familiarity and I felt an inexplicable relief to be in the land of my grandmother's roots.

December 12

> *Sharing a room with Rosemary who used to go to Headington is not exactly a developing process for me spiritually. But I must remember you can learn from everybody.*

My experience of the kibbutz was like a kind of homecoming. I slept in a bed in a bedroom, had a work routine and ate regular meals. I ate in the community dining room sitting on a chair at a table with cutlery and crockery, instead of sitting on the ground eating with my hands. I had arrived in a time-tested mature community that had order and ease despite the rumblings of the recent conflict.

The dining room, or cheder ochel, was a large hall right in the centre of the kibbutz. A long table covered in numerous dishes of wholesome food stood just inside the door. On that first day I watched people ahead of me in the line heaping up their plates from great bowls of salad, chicken, chips and slices of freshly harvested eggplants fried in olive oil. I poured a creamy sauce made from tahini, lemon juice and garlic all over my plate and sat down on a long table surrounded by loud exuberant talk, shouts and laughter. The conversation stopped briefly as I was welcomed, then continued in the same lively manner in a mixture of Hebrew and English. I felt bewildered as I adjusted to the domesticity, to using cutlery, sitting inside, and eating at a table. I was thrown by the directness of the kibbutzniks. People reached across the table in mid-sentence for things, or spoke loudly past me to someone further up the table. I was taken aback. I had been taught so-called correct English table manners at school by a prim teacher. At this table there were no pleases or thankyous.

After some days of watching people I began to appreciate their immediacy and liveliness. They weren't being rude, they just related in a different way. There was a realness and directness, and as time went on, the polite table manners I'd been taught seemed stiff with artificial courtesy. Gathering for meals was an important aspect of the communal life of the kibbutz. The banter, exchanges, and arguments all added to building and maintaining community.

Another reason the kibbutz felt like home was Rosemary. I met her minutes after my lift had dropped me at the entrance of the kibbutz. She had been at the same school as me though I couldn't remember her. She came running pell-mell down the gravel drive towards me, waving and calling my name, arriving at my feet bursting with excitement. A sturdy figure with a round face, hair in all directions and a huge grin. It was weird to come to a strange land and hear a too familiar English voice. Rosemary enthusiastically told me we were to share a room as we were both English.

I listened to her as we walked up the drive and my heart sank. I had been stretched and amazed by so many different people and ideas since I left home. Now suddenly I was to be living with someone who was just too familiar. I was coming to life, and felt miles away from the alienation I'd felt at school. The last thing I wanted was anything that reminded me of that atmosphere.

I judged Rosemary because she had flourished in the environment I hated. Only later I realised it was what she represented, not who she was that I was reacting to.

A few days after I arrived, I told my new kibbutznik friends, Yanai, Shilo and Tobi about my recent discovery of having a Jewish grandmother. We were standing outside the cheder ochel after supper.

With a flourish of his hands that I noticed were bent and misshapen, Yanai said:

'So now you are really Jewish!'

'Well it's not me, I'm not Jewish, it was my grandmother.'

'No, no, it's more. If she is Jewish so is your mother and so are you. You inherit it from the women. It's a line. You didn't know this?'

'No, is that really how it is?'

'You think we would make it up?'

They all laughed at my surprise.

'We must have a special ceremony for you to make you properly Jewish now you are in Israel.'

I must have looked anxious but the three men laughed again and Shilo put his hand on my shoulder and smiled and said they were joking. These young Israelis had more serious life and death issues to deal with. Later I heard Shilo had shrapnel wounds in his hands from the recent war. All the young people I spent time with dreaded being called up.

December 13

> *1st days' work – oranges. I liked it. It's easy work compared to Crete. Coffee break in the morning. Juice break in the afternoon. They're a good crowd.*

It was a sweet relief to be in a much larger group where I felt more anonymous and fluid after the intensity and rawness of life on Crete. No one preached any spiritual doctrine at me. I was free to think and act as I wanted as long as I did my daily share of work. Yet the principles of sharing and fairness had followed me there, as the kibbutzim were founded in socialist ideas of equality, the selfsame principles that Pierre and Eddie so passionately espoused. But here was a bigger scale: I was one of 39 volunteers in a community of 300 permanent members.

I wrote home:

> *It's incredible what they've done. It was started in '37 with a small group of settlers. The land was just rock and dryness*

but they attacked it and planted all the trees themselves. It was quite a hard time for them then, but there is still just as much energy put into the kibbutz now.

As volunteers we were all given kibbutz "parents", and were invited to eat at their houses once a week. I found mine dry and severe and I felt awkward sitting with them at their kitchen table as I knew hardly any Hebrew and they little English. Despite feeling tense I managed to ask them about the early days. With fierce pride, in broken English, they told me they were there from the beginning, describing the harsh work, the laborious toil on a rocky hillside to build the first foundations. They would not say more, maybe because of the language barrier, or because the memory was too grim.

The very first pioneering settlements in Israel were built in 1909 in a bleak land that was either rocky or swampy. My grandmother was born in 1900 in London, and I wondered if anyone in her family had travelled out to be part of the movement building new kibbutzim. Most settlers had no farming experience and living collectively was a practical solution initially; the commune philosophy developed later. My kibbutz "parents" were likely to have been just as inexperienced when they arrived to work on the bare land of what was to be their kibbutz in the 1930s, and would have learnt as they went along. They wore their title of "founders" with hard-won pride. It was a pioneer period when self-sacrifice of the individual was made for the sake of the ideal. In the beginning there was a wish for equality with the Arabs. Joseph Baratz, a pioneer of the kibbutz movement who fathered the first child to be born on one, called for justness, not domination.

December 14

> *Worked with the lemons. I enjoyed it. They are such a beautiful fruit. Shape, smell and colour. Barry, an Australian Kibbutznik told us a lot about the kibbutz. He lives here permanently. I went to have tea with him today with his grandparents.*

There was a rhythm to the day that was satisfying after three months of living with no structure or plans. I loved the daily ride on the open trailer out to the pardes, the orchards. I picked oranges, lemons and grapefruit. I was offered other jobs, but for four whole months I mainly picked oranges. I felt at home in the citrus orchards. Even now when I drink tea and eat oranges at the same time, the combination of those tastes takes me straight back there, together with the rough cotton work clothes on my skin.

'I never see any children, where are they?', I asked Tobi one day in the cheder ochel. It was odd not to see little ones running around.

'In the children's house,' he answered, smiling at my surprised face. 'Children don't live with their parents. They all stay together in their own house. It's how it goes here. Same for me when I was growing up.'

I was impressed. Such a totally different life to mine. The young Israelis seemed stronger and freer than anyone I knew in England and I was making friends with kibbutzniks my age who had experienced this upbringing.

The author picking oranges in kibbutz work clothes

I wrote a long excited letter home:

I find the young Israelis really incredible. They seem very open – very independent, just incredibly real. Its partly because of a naivety. The fact they have never lived outside of a kibbutz, they have always had the security of a great big home, never becoming 'corrupted' with the evils outside! They have always lived on the basis of sharing and everything they produce and make. As they have had the same allowance as everyone else, feeling of jealousy and competition don't seem to exist. They have a much better life than Israeli children living outside – so no responsibilities, and security with a good free education. Enough food and clothes, but not enough to be spoilt. When they are born they go into the children house. The mother has 6 weeks off work so she can go and feed it. The baby house here has just been built. It is very new and modern. Then the children gradually progress into bigger baby houses until they begin school, then all the children sleep in the school house. The children can go and stay in their parents house if they want to, but parents and children are always happy about it. They go round for tea with their parents but there is no set time for visiting outside school or work. At about 14 the children do about 3 hours work on the kibbutz as well as school work (though not so many hours) and homework. At 18 they go into the army for 3 years. After they return to the kibbutz it is up to their parents to let them go if they wish, otherwise they stay on the kibbutz. Today many of them want to leave. The system appears hard because it is so different but it really is effective. There is very little disharmony or adverse feelings in the young Israelis about the way things are run and no crime or suicides. There is something like one of two cases of theft and suicide in the whole history of the kibbutz.

Obviously it can't be perfect because people are human. For instance it is forbidden to get drunk but many of the young Kibbutzniks drink a lot. Every family has the same allowance, differing of course to the number of children etc, but a few cars do exist here which are privately owned. It would be impossible to own a car on the allowance they are given. When someone wants to become a full kibbutznik usually they are meant to give over everything they own, but there are, for some reason, some exceptions.

For the moment it is quiet as most of the men are fighting. Three men from this kibbutz were killed in this war and a few injured. Rosemary was here when it broke out. They had to go down in the bomb shelter a couple of times, but nothing else was effected. All the volunteers except for some Swedish girls stayed on here during the war. They have just started giving Hebrew lessons but they are not very good. I think I'll get a book out on my own.

The principle of equality was a given until the 1970s. Until that point kibbutzniks didn't own tools or even clothing individually and if gifts or income arrived from outside the kibbutz they were automatically given to the common fund. When I arrived it was beginning to change; if someone was given the chance to visit a relative and go abroad, arguments would arise at members' meetings. But these internal rumblings went over my head for I was unfurling into a wonderful place of elation.

December 23

Tonight is the first time I have really written anything much since I've been in the kibbutz. In the last two weeks I've been happier than ever before – rather, I've had moments of joy that I never knew I could experience, but all through getting to a state of mind that centred on the fact that people are the most important thing.

Something woke up in my heart singing with happiness. As the days passed in my new home I felt more and more at ease. I loved the bright, sunny mornings driving out to the pardes, laughing and talking in the trailer. I felt accepted and appreciated by my new friends, and as we worked together each day a warm glow nestled in my heart and grew. All my physical needs were met; we had pocket money and bought essentials from the little kibbutz volunteer shop. For other wants or needs Jerusalem was close by with its winding market streets stuffed with marvellous weavings, clothes and ornaments that other volunteers had visited. But I had no urge to go. I felt so complete on the kibbutz and there was nothing else I wanted. I loved the fact that money played no part in my life – just the simple exchange of labour for food and lodging. I didn't have to search for work, think about money, or even deal with my obsessive feelings for Pierre. Like most teenage obsessions it was over the day I slipped away from Crete.

I began to experience a sustained joyfulness. This feeling of harmony was inside me, not attached to anyone else, or enhanced by dope of which I was taking little. It was a huge relief to feel embraced in the bosom of the kibbutz that did not expect me to be anything other than I was. So different from the tough times on Crete. The supportive inclusion, the ease and generosity, and a sense I had landed in my spiritual home in the land of Israel, all served to create a transfiguration inside me, a rare state, where my mind stopped and every second was a dance of joy.

Words can inevitably elevate memory, but my diary entry for this fortnight was scant. Being happier than ever before was the briefest report about an extraordinary aliveness. I was experiencing something untellable which baffled my pen. There have been one or two short times in my life when joyful synchronicities fell into my life like bright waterfalls, but nothing had ever lasted as long as this two week continuum of bliss. Suspended in a state of elation I found I knew what people were going to say before they spoke and who I would meet before I met them. I also had a clear sense of myself stretching forwards in time.

In my diary I wrote to my future self:

If you are reading now and you looked in the mirror – maybe you could see the old eyes of her though the changes. I was really someone else in this book. Everyday the changes go on and sometimes I'm not there for them so they slow up waiting patiently for me, but other times when I'm at one then I take off. If you could hear the rain now – it suddenly came down in a rush, running down the roof, through the trees, down the path, singing so freely. Its been raining for four days – tonight it started again with growls and flashes, so powerful. I love the storm. Before I never noticed it.

I felt I was riding a huge loving wave that I was one with, describing it in my diary as "the changes". When I wasn't "there for them" I felt as if "they" waited till I caught up. Maybe what I meant was when I began to think about what was happening to me I lost the connection. But when I did stop and feel, I was able to shift into a place of being "at one" again and re-enter the experience.

I don't want to try and remember each day's happenings. Time just melts days into days so dated diaries are useless here for me.

I broke out of the confines of writing every day in my diary. Marking time felt meaningless and my writing flowed across the dated pages, ignoring them. Up until now on my journey I had reported life as it happened day by day. In Crete my writing was a root of security amidst swirling emotions and challenging relationships. Now I no longer felt the need for that intimate relationship with my diary, daily detailing the elucidations of my inner world. I felt a palpable sense of belonging in Israel, held and nourished in a community of warmth. I felt completely safe, and I let go into a magical experience.

Things keep happening that aren't just coincidences. There is so much meaning in the weather, the wind, things that are said and Tom. His superstitions are too overpowering for me to go along with completely but...

Everything felt completely alive. My connections with people felt vital and dynamic, yet peaceful as well. After work friends would drop by to the room I shared with Rosemary and we would chat, sitting outside under the trees or on the floor of our simple room.

Sometimes when people speak they say something that is different. I feel a force of another nature is speaking through them, not strong, but hinting. Oh words, so plastic, so dead. I want so much to be able to read this at any time in the future and not to laugh at it. How can I write down what has happened? The answer is there. I can't. And why this need for a record – why this need to be able to remember? Maybe that is still part of the shit that is still covering me. Interesting that this space of time being the most unfucked and clean and clear I have ever been, also went with not writing. Thus... all the things I write must be pretty confused, not coming from 'me' – the truth.

There was one volunteer who especially affirmed my rarefied state. This was Tom, a tall American with long hair who had lived with a spiritual teacher in India. He was unhurried and relaxed, easy to be with.

Today Saturday, I woke up at 2.00pm hearing Tom's voice through a sleepy consciousness. He wanted to know if someone would walk with him. Later it was. I was still in my dreams. He seemed so together. The Bedouin postman came along on a muddy grey horse. We watched him trot towards us from the other side of the field. They were so transient at a distance. Always fading into the sunlight on the grass and the trees beyond.

We walked out to a dry wadi, a river bed nearby, following the winding white path between strange, sculptural, white rocks jutting dramatically out of the sand, creating an intense jagged line against the vibrant blue skyline above us. It was windless, hot and still. I loved the atmosphere there. We were a mile or two away from the kibbutz, with just the occasional goat bell and the call of bedouins to their flocks.

Tom stopped to sit on a rock and looked thoughtfully down through the wadi.

'We're all expanding Carrie, though most folks don't know it. The energy on the planet is changing and waking up. Everything is being made possible.'

The heat shimmered in the stillness as his words drifted over to me.

'I can feel it. Everything feels more connected and alive.'

'But of course talking about it just puts it on the mental level.'

'I don't feel like I lose it when I talk about it.'

Tom sat looking at me steadily.

'We're talking about infinity here. That can't be named.

Words mean time and space.'

'But I don't feel like I'm in a mental state. All I know is I feel different all the time here whether I'm talking or not talking. It's different to anything I've felt before. Since I've been in Israel something has happened, as if I don't know myself any more. But that feels good, like I'm meeting a new clear self.'

'Far out! You're dropping your old self, and the more you give it up, you'll have it all. You sure do seem high on bliss!

He laughed. 'You can't turn back now. Bodhisattva is not far off. Huge floods are coming to take the evil off the planet as only love can remain.'

Tom was being weird again. I respected a lot of what he said but when he took off in a prophetic voice he lost me. I was silent then I brought the conversation back to his experiences of meditation. Tom had been on silent retreat for a year in India and had circumnavigated his inner world more than many. He spoke about the challenge of the mind in spiritual practice, which, having only meditated sporadically, I only half understood. I couldn't go along with everything he said, but he seemed to understand my spiritual experiences and he felt like a kindred spirit.

Life was far more relaxed than life in Crete but I still needed time to myself. One day I decided not to get back up on the open truck to head back for lunch, and I stayed behind in the pardes, the citrus groves that were a twenty minute ride away from the main kibbutz. It was a still, hot day, the ground shimmering with heat. I sat on the ground in the middle of a straight wide path between symmetrical rows of trees.

I noticed a movement and looked up. Walking very, very slowly towards me was a horse. It made no sound on the grass as it lifted its feet, placing them back down again with utmost care. I had never seen a horse near the pardes and was startled. It was clearly intent in coming towards me, and was walking in a straight line between the trees in a kind of slow ceremonial gait. Then, appearing from behind a tree in the densely planted row came a donkey, who, as if choreographed, came abreast of the horse and both together walked slowly and evenly towards me. There was no one around and as they came ever nearer and nearer I was entranced. They were bridle-less, perhaps exhausted by the heat, and they stopped and started several times but always more or less together as they came even closer. Their gentle progression along the straight path flanked by orange trees felt ritualistic. I looked in the horse's eyes and for a moment they both stopped. The three of us were held together in a magical spell in the still afternoon. I felt a calmness and ease in our contact that made us strangely equal. I was mesmerised, and I felt my heart open softly in joy.

When they were a few feet from me, a familiar rumble of the tractor bringing the volunteers back made the animals start, and they turned and went swiftly off through the thick shadowy lines of trees. This unexpected meeting with the animal kingdom melted away our differences, transcended who we were as human and animal. I had received a miraculous gift that I stowed quietly away in my heart.

This gift from the animals was a precursor to contacting my own animal body, for a day later I was initiated into a practice that would ignite a passionate interest in me. Tom had trained in Hatha Yoga in India and was offering a class. I gathered this was something new for the kibbutz and it was allocated a rather hidden-away room. I walked along the leafy path past the children's house with its colourful artwork stuck across the windows and entered a dark narrow room with mats laid out in a neat row on the floor. Several people were in the process of getting down onto the floor. I joined them and lay waiting expectantly, staring up at the ceiling. Tom stood not saying anything. I wondered why he was waiting, but then his deep gravelly voice guided us gently and caressingly into a posture:

'Bring your body into sitting and notice if you can what moves you make to get there.'

This was my first experience of being asked to notice my movement. It was strange to observe myself doing something I did every day unthinkingly. I lifted my head, and then rested on my elbows for a bit before I sat up, which felt nice.

'Now sit up straight and imagine a thread coming out of the top of your head. Breathe in, and on the outbreath sense your spine extending and lifting up. Yes, good. Do this for two more deep breaths. There's no rush, let your breathing deepen. Now the next time you breathe out, gently lean towards your feet. If you can't reach them, hold your ankles. Hold that position and breathe deeply and see if you can extend the stretch on each outbreath.'

Making the slow stretch was a revelation. I had never moved so gradually before. I felt a peaceful sensation spreading inside my body. My muscles responded gratefully to this treatment after lugging heavy orange bags around all day. I could feel they were working in a very different way. I loved the feeling of stillness, yet physically extending and lengthening at the same time. I understood I was not trying to reach a goal, but to work with my own body's limit, feeling its edge and breathing into it.

'Now return to neutral. That means lying on your backs with your arms on the floor by your sides. See if you can completely let go. Allow your body to rest. See if you can stop your thoughts and be peaceful.'

We were doing movement for its own sake and it made me feel good. I remembered how much I had loved creative dance at junior school until the teacher decided to hold a performance. She had called it "Caroline's Nightmare". I had to wear my white nightie and move swiftly around on the stage avoiding lots of black, leotarded little demons. Wearing my nightie in front of the whole school was excruciatingly embarrassing and the experience had not fostered my love of movement.

In Tom's class, as my body took on new and different shapes, I started breathing more deeply and began to notice different areas of my body. Lying down in neutral I felt my back in firm reassuring contact with the floor. My legs were pleasantly heavy, my feet turned outwards and I started noticing the small of my back relaxing a bit more after each posture.

So far pain was the only thing that had made me give my full attention to my body. Now instead of urgent attention, there was a gentle slow spreading of awareness.

'Let your body totally relax. You need the neutral pose to let what you've just done leave your body so there's no trace of it left in your muscles. Then the next pose will be really fresh.'

In those neutral times, I felt I was resting in a way I never had before. There was a spacious quality that felt timeless. But I was not spacing out as I did when smoking dope. This was different. I was present in my body and by relaxing after each position, it seemed that my body was digesting and integrating the effect of the stretch. I was waking up my body awareness.

Tom gave equal emphasis and value to these resting positions as he did to the actual poses or asanas. I had not stopped and simply felt like this before. It was extraordinary and lovely. When lying still I imagined the posture I had just held sliding out of my body into the floor. The sensations in my body in those minutes of repose are what I remember. Yet the pleasure of that letting-go was accomplished through the deep engagement of my muscles in the preceding stretch. I was experiencing the relationship of movement to stillness.

Each week I went along to the narrow room hungry for more. I felt a satisfaction from extending my muscles and my body was easing more and more into the stretches. I lay happily in neutral, basking in a new sensation of bodily calm. At school I had not been able to touch my toes, but in a few weeks that changed and I could. Each class before he said anything Tom stood in silence, but I stopped waiting for him to speak, luxuriating instead in the feeling of simply arriving in my body on the floor. I relished my new awareness of movement and sensation and felt as if my body had been waiting for this. It was an introduction into a relationship with my body that would become my life-long practice and work.

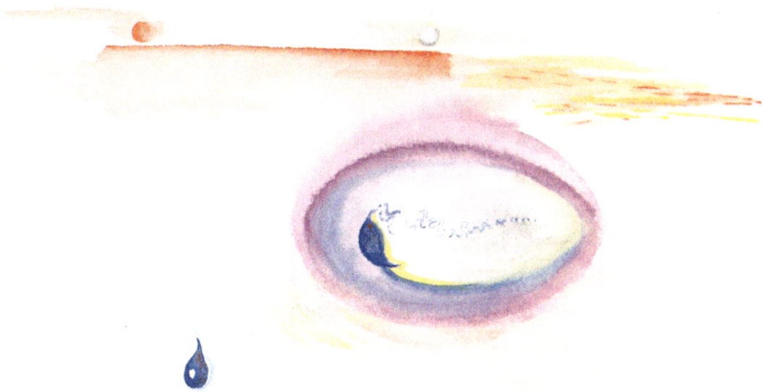

As far back as the Greek islands I had envisioned being in Bethlehem for Christmas. Feeling so wonderfully high, I fantasized that being in that sacred birthplace would be a crowning of my experience. The timing was perfect, the year was fluidly coming to its close, and I was full of the happiest days of my life. I eagerly hitched to the town with Anja and Lena, two Dutch volunteers. Although I didn't think of myself as Christian, I believed in Christ and his birth, and to visit his holy birthplace on Christmas Eve felt momentous. But the wind was knocked sharply from my sails. I had expected it to be a holy experience but I was wrong. It was the turning of my high tide of happiness.

Writing home I tried to explain:

In the back of my mind I was expecting Bethlehem to be like it was all those years ago, but 'Manger Square' where everyone gathered, resembled St Paul's a little in size, with people of all kinds walking around. Loudspeakers blaring out jazzed up carols. A little Arab boy stole my drum – a little bongo drum I had bought – which really brought across the fact that 'Good will among men' is something of an illusion in 1973. We found a convent called The White Sisters and stayed there the night, which was like a haven in a way, feeling tired from all the nights festivities. It was so strange coming back to the kibbutz.

The reality was a shock. I had hoped for a sacred celebration, something that held beauty and meaning, thinking it inevitable in such a special place. But the event was superficial and crass. Crestfallen, I had stopped for a moment in crowded Manger Square, laying my new drum at my feet. In a flash it had gone. With it went the rest of my euphoria, shattering the blissful state that had blessed and transported me. When I returned to the kibbutz I felt changed, and my re-entry into the community was painfully difficult. When I had left it a few days earlier I felt transcendent. Returning there I felt squashed inside a small cracked shell – all I felt I was. The expanded me had gone. I didn't know where to put my eyes or even how to relate.

After the downer at Bethlehem, I crashed. Maybe it had been just too intense to take – I'm strong but only human.

Also, together with self-awareness of a pure kind, another awareness had crept in – the superior me. Nobody else has climbed up the stairs, only I can give love, and, I have been chosen for something. This is what maybe brought me down in a foolish swirling heap on the dead leaves. I've been up and down, so high and then so so depressed.

I had started to think I was more enlightened than anyone else. Perhaps an inevitable desire in the magical state I was in, but I berated myself and blamed it for my comedown.

All the people I loved before seem to be turning back on me in my weakness demanding a development of my attentions. I feel at the moment I'm not strong enough to keep cool and consistent. I thought there wasn't much further down to go but I was wrong. Later I listened to Lena playing piano in the big dark empty cheder ochel. It was beautiful but I couldn't dance even though I wanted to. Fuck my inhibitions. Then confusion and insecurity for the rest of the evening – people seemed to turn into lusting werewolves – I seemed to turn into stone.

The days of my enlightenment were over. A black cloud enveloped me and people felt demanding and predatory. Before Christmas I was wide open with no margins, meeting all with an open heart. Now I was weak and shaky, yet people expected the same woman who poured out love and warmth. I could not. They didn't know I had changed and I had no words to explain. I had only just enough of myself for myself. Feeling invaded, I retreated to my room.

Generally couldn't handle anything or anyone this evening. I was meant to meet Barry's grandparents today for Shabbat dinner which is formal and more special than usual. I waited for them and freaked when someone talked to me. Why do I feel so weak I could be knocked down with a feather?

I was relieved that Rosemary asked nothing of me. She didn't comment on the fact I had withdrawn from socialising in the evenings and stayed in our room silently buried in a book. She was quietly sensitive to my change of mood and gave me space. She still reminded me of home and my stifled time at school and I still reacted to anyone or anything that reminded me of that world, but it was less, and I no longer felt impatient with her or found her too cautious. She told me it was dangerous to look at your own eyes in the mirror for too long. It was a strange thing to say but I accepted her reality and fears.

I began to feel sorry about a joke I had played on her with some of the volunteers soon after I arrived. In high jinx we had teased her about being so formal and British. Late one night when she was fast asleep we crept into the room and all carried her bed with her asleep on it out of the door towards the central lawn. We only got as far as the doorway when she woke up and angrily demanded we put her back inside the room. There was a lot of joking made at her expense. One evening I brought it up and apologised, but she brushed it off laughing at the idea of herself being paraded round the lawn high up on her bed.

Although sensitive to my reticence, she couldn't resist

telling naff jokes, and still low, I actually found them a comfort. She was so non-spiritual I thought, yet she was an ordinary middle-class English girl – just like me in fact, and in my insecure state this sameness was reassuring. Unlike the others, Rosemary accepted my low mood, which made it easier to accept myself. Just being herself, she helped me be myself, the nothing special, ordinary me. I was adjusting to the loss of my amazing experience and being together, often reading in silence, helped me through. She was, I realised over time, the perfect room-mate.

> *Since then I've been up and down in small stages; round and round, over and over, happy and sad, stupid and wise, getting into all superficialities of life and not so superficial things.*

I had another friend who gave quiet company. John was on the boat heading for Israel and was part of the little community living on the beach in Cyprus. He had made his own way to Israel and got a job working in a cement factory in Natanya. We met again in Bethlehem at Christmas. I was standing in Manger Square seconds after a little Arab boy had streaked off with my new drum. Feeling dejected I turned around and John walked up. I told him life was good on the kibbutz, better than making cement, and he said he would write and ask to volunteer. Back in Netanya he waited for a letter of acceptance, gave in his notice, then walked south for five days through the Israeli countryside. On the last day, as he entered the orange orchards in the dusty scented night, he turned to see, for the first and only time, the comet Kohoutek shining in the sky.

Despite my previous reaction to being with English people, I started to enjoy the familiarity, and I enjoyed spending time with Rosemary and John. Rosemary was clear about not being a hippy or smoking dope. I appreciated her honesty and cheerfulness and she had grown into a loyal friend. After sharing a room together for two months, her warmth and humour got through to me. I had regaled her with tales of my travels, of my delight in sleeping in nature, and the freedom I felt on the road. She was eager to try out the same kind of travelling and asked if we could take a trip together. We decided to hitch the hundred miles north to the Sea of Galilee and set off one weekend.

We knew it was safe to hitch round Israel and we got friendly rides in army trucks. We travelled up the west coast to Haifa and then up to Rosh Hanikra on the Lebanese border, a beautiful place high up on the cliffs. Then across to Safad, an artist's colony, the highest city in Israel.

The second evening we were on the road hitching late. We finally gave up on a ride, the roads were empty and dark so we scrambled up into a wood by the side of the road. It was a dense tangle so we only got a few feet in and crawled into our sleeping bags. Just as we had lain down, a growling rumble vibrated through the wood.

'Rosemary,' I whispered.

What is it? What's happening?'

'I don't know but it's so horrid. What are those lights?'

Powerful beams of light flashed across the tree trunks above us. The silence of the wood with a distant owl hooting had dramatically changed. A thunderous grinding sound reverberated violently through my body. I was terrified. I saw Rosemary sit up and stare out pale-faced under the lights. Fearfully I waited for her to say something.

'They're tanks. There's one going past right now. There's lots of them I think. Ugh! it's so loud.'

It was a long convoy of trucks and tanks going very slowly. I felt tiny and insignificant lying only feet away from such a faceless lumbering arsenal. We whispered to each other as we lay prone in the darkness while their lights blazed across the tree trunks. It went on and on, taking over an hour to go past us in the wood. Then finally the noise dropped intensity and began to fade. As darkness returned we lay awake until the sound had completely died away. Finally there was just the wind sighing over the tops of the trees. Later we discovered there was fighting not far away in the Golan Heights. I wondered if Rosemary was praying in those scary moments like I was, but I didn't ask. I was enjoying her company, but subtle mannerisms in both of us were reinstating my cloak of English reserve. I was influenced by the atmosphere of being with a more traditional English girl and was unknowingly shutting down the open and receptive explorative state I had freed up in myself.

But in the morning birds were singing and the sun was out and we were happy as we chatted together walking along the road. We got a lift through Tiberias and round the bottom of the Sea of Galilee to Kibbutz En Gev where we had decided to sleep in the grounds. Walking down to the shore that evening we recalled the familiar bible stories of events that had taken place there. Jesus walking on the water, calming the storm, and the disciples and the miraculous catch of fish.

Feeling shy to speak about spiritual experience, what we might feel there, I stood silently with Rosemary by the water's edge, hoping for something magical to happen. We stared out across the huge lake, thirteen miles across. It was wild and unspoilt, but the light faded, bringing nothing special. I was hoping to experience at the least a healing atmosphere but I was disappointed. We flattened the rushes to make space to sleep, unrolled our sleeping bags and lay down to a quieter night's rest.

I took my little sewing kit everywhere. My long skirt easily caught on thorns or twigs, and the next morning, sitting on my sleeping bag by the reeds beside the water I took it out of my rucksack to mend a new tear. I left it lying in the rushes. Despite my belief in non-attachment,

I loved my few possessions, and losing my beloved tin with its pretty leather marquetry was a wrench. It sat by the bank of the holy sea, like a gift to honour the holy place.

The next day we had a lift all the way to Jerusalem along the Jordan River and through Jericho. We arrived home on Shabbat in time for a lively Purim party with everyone in fancy dress with side shows, bumper cars and magicians for the children.

By the time I left the kibbutz Rosemary and I were good friends, both of us seeing beyond our outer differences and valuing the person inside. I grew to respect her clarity and feistiness. She always gave as good as she got and stuck up for herself. A few years later I drove from London to York in my old and slow Austin A40 to a fancy dress party in her grand new home in York.

Jerusalem

On the Mount of Olives it was like a return to the Cretan scene. I had lunch with an Arab family. I fell in the mud and dried out over their stove. They all sat cross-legged. The two little boys pushing into the centre nearer the fire and the grandmother picking up crumbs from the coloured rugs on the floor, and hit her grandsons round the ears now and then. We drunk two cups of coffee and ate toast and rice covered with leaves. They treated me like a guest. I wish I could have been more like them.

My next trip away from the kibbutz was to Jerusalem. I wanted to visit a holy place to put another famous Christian legend into physical reality, hoping this time it would be uplifting. The Mount of Olives, like many others, was a familiar name for me, but still only a place in a story. On the bus I day-dreamed about a idyllic hill graced with flowers; when the ancient walls came into view, I hopped off and walked quickly through the old city, ignoring the entreaties of the market stall sellers. A couple of American tourists offered directions, and I soon found myself at the foot of a sloping hill. This was it. The ground was uneven and rough, a few straggly trees looked sad in the grey light, but I climbed up slowly, trying to feel the atmosphere. It started to rain and I turned back, but my foot slid and I fell in the mud. Struggling to stand, I slipped even more, plastering my skirt and smearing my arms in wet sludge.

I felt someone looking at me and looked up to see a

small dark-skinned old woman beckoning from a low doorway. I struggled over to an unassuming circular hut where she stood motioning me inside with fast movements of her fingers. Her crinkled-up eyes were dark, but she welcomed me warmly into her dwelling, indicating I should sit on the floor by the fire in the centre where her two little grandsons stared up at me. She was a Palestinian grandmother, and she treated me like an honoured guest. With my seat on the soft carpet laid on the earth, the warmth of the fire, the kettle steaming above it and the rain out through the open doorway, I was taken back to my time in Cyprus living on the beach sharing everything with friends. I wanted to feel equal with these people too, to feel one of the family, but the old lady's dignified reserve conveyed otherwise. I was welcome, but I was different.

After drying out for an hour or so enjoying the warmth and welcome, I wanted to give them something. Bev, my close friend at school, had given me a crucifix before I left. It was all I had to give, so I stood up, undid the chain from round my neck and offered it to the grandmother.

After the peaceful time sitting round their fire with few words, seeing the cross in my hand she jumped up shouting loudly in Arabic, strong guttural sounds, gesticulating at me, refusing to take it. The little boys jumped up and ran around the room excited and noisy. But I insisted, feeling it was right to give them a gift. Suddenly she went quiet and took it.

Afterwards I was terrified in a big lonely square. Arabs shouting out of smoky little cafes and one camel standing under a tree looking at me silently.

I offered the crucifix because I was immersed in a hippie worldview where all spiritual paths were equal, all leading to the same Source. I didn't want to accept we had differences and I was blind to the incongruity of my gift. I gave no weight to the idea that religious symbols were the possession of separate religions. My naive absorption in spiritual harmony left me unaware I might offend. I believed people were more important than beliefs, and I was unconscious of the religious discrepancy of my gift.

My meeting with the Arab woman and her family was another rich encounter I had come to expect. It flowed past in time as life continued on.

I was getting closer to new friends. Anja was one of the two Dutch volunteers, who was tall, quiet and serious. We had short conversations and I liked her. She used few words, was simple and direct. We had picked in the same tree many times and one day in February we were up our ladders talking through the prickly branches of a lemon tree.

'So Carrie,' Anja said, 'would you like to do something special for our friendship?'

Her round face smiled at me through a green network of leaves.

'What sort of special thing are you thinking about?' I

asked, reaching up for an extra-large sun-warmed lemon above my head.

'It is something I have done before with friends at home in Amsterdam. Both of us write two lists. On the first list we write the things we don't like about our friend, and the next list we write all the things we do like about them. Then we tell our friend what we have written and they tell us.'

My hand cradling the large lemon stopped in mid-air as I stared at it. I had explored many possibilities of friendship on my journey and I felt pretty free in how I related. But Anja was challenging boundaries I hadn't even thought about. I'd never dreamed I could say what I didn't like about someone, let alone for that to be ok. My notions of what I thought possible and acceptable in relating to people were turned upside down.

She went on explaining her exercise as she steadily went on picking: 'If we really do like each other then we must be honest as well. Real friendship means really being honest. Do you agree?'

Even to say what I liked about someone felt risky. But I was not one to say no to such a challenge, especially from someone with such depth of character.

We agreed to meet in my room that evening. Rosemary was out and we sat on the floor and wrote our lists in silence. I chewed the end of my pen as I struggled to write down what I found difficult about Anja. I was fighting off generations of people-pleasing patterns. Hesitatingly I wrote down 'aloof,' then 'cool.' It took me time even to realise what I didn't like in Anja as my tendency was to avoid these thoughts about friends. It was a hard task. When we read our lists out to each other from our bits of paper, Anja's list of my faults and positive qualities was much longer than mine. I realised that, like me, Anja was also tense. I flinched at what I was told, but this tough honesty cut through all my pretend niceness and made me feel more alive. When we stood up I felt proud to have been able to meet the test as one of Anja's friends.

Anja was my age, but the ideas she proffered out of her silences were mind-opening for me. We would climb up on the water tower and sit on the top taking in the view over the kibbutz and the rolling land beyond. I was talking at length about ego and my attempts to lessen mine. We were both silent for some time. Then, quietly, Anja asked:

'Have you ever given someone a present and not said it was from you?'

'No,' I confessed, guessing what was coming.

'If you are serious about letting your ego go, then you need to try it don't you think?'

So later I chose one of the volunteers, picked some flowers, and crept round to their room when they were in the dining room and left them on their pillow. I had strange mixed feelings. Part of me wanted appreciation and another part was excited to think about their surprise. It was a regular act for Anja.

As I recovered from both my high state and my following downer, I returned to spiritual questioning and caught myself trying to return to my high state.

> *But another thought as "Be Here Now" ideas come infiltrating gently, strongly through – it doesn't matter as every transference is for the better. I'll learn from my negative states. And thus, stop trying to get high, because then it all becomes as ridiculous as it sounds – try to get high. Just as ridiculous as trying to do it artificially ? Will it ever come if you try and reach out for it? I suppose not. Like the man who tastes gold after being a beggar. He then craves after it and eventually dies in the misery and unhappiness of being a rich man. So, and thus the moral… But I must stay awake as well.*

There was a German volunteer my age called Axel with fluffy fair hair and wire-rimmed specs. He sat on my bed and read "The Little Prince" out loud. I lay on the floor below him, letting his quiet sonorous voice drift across me. He gave me a copy of "The Prophet" by Khalil Gibran and I wrote swathes of it out in my journal.

And in the sweetness of friendship let there

be laughter, and sharing of pleasures.

For in the dew of little things the heart

finds its morning and is refreshed.

I had asked my friends on the kibbutz to write their

thoughts in my journal. This was a bigger book acquired from the kibbutz shop as my tiny 1973 diary was complete. Sophie had drawn doodles, but no one else offered except for Axel who wrote he wanted me to "please tame him", as the little prince said to the flower. He felt like a child to me, a little brother. The love between us was all heart, uncurling like shy green leaves. He was a fragile and tender man.

All my close friends on the kibbutz were unique and different to anyone I knew in England and they brought out new qualities and ideas in my own character map. Sophie amazed and delighted me. She was an American volunteer a year older than me who had been on the kibbutz on and off for a year. She and Yanai were lovers and lived together. As his hands had been so wounded she helped him dress and eat. I was so touched by her and her easy and generous love for Yanai. She said the intimate things she did for his care were just part of loving him. She was completely unfazed and the most open person I had met. In her relaxed American drawl she talked about sex with ease, how she used contraception, treating me as a mature woman friend. She was only a year older than me, but I felt like a complete innocent in comparison. She had a tall and fierce big sister called Ellen who was completely the opposite, critical and stiff. She seemed uncomfortable on the kibbutz, and showed her disapproval of Sophie's easy ways. Perhaps she had been sent to try and keep an eye on her. Sophie completely ignored her, seemingly totally unaffected. In our chats lazing around on the communal lawn, Sophie confided she was going to learn Blackjack once she was back in the States, from an uncle who knew how to win.

Maybe if I could clean myself of my psychological complexities like the physical restraint it would be better.

I had held back from amorous approaches but criticised myself for my restraint. I felt a pressure from my self-judgement that said I was too complicated and uptight. One night I was on my way out of the cheder ochel when Nuri called my name. He was standing by the door looking at me. He was one of the kibbutzniks I hung around with: a solidly built, chunky man with thick curly black hair. I stood near the door wondering what he wanted. People were walking out between us, but as I looked at him I felt rooted into stillness by his dark eyes focussed on mine. My mind flashed up the figures in a Massacio painting I had been fascinated by in A level art history. The painter had emphasised their solid forms so three-dimensionally they looked like living sculptures. There was the same sculptural solidity to Nuri standing there – something of the air of an old testament prophet. I noticed his wide shoulders as I stood looking back, shy under his long stare. People were walking out past us but Nuri totally ignored them. Then he walked closer to me and without a smile said:

'I want you.'

The simplicity of his entreaty penetrated through the layers of my good-girl middle-class upbringing, unmasking me. This earthy directness in the bright light of day stays clear in my memory. The rest is muffled in darkness. Climbing up the wooden steps to Nuri's treehouse dwelling and walking over to the bed on the floor is all I can remember.

I had no reticence about my naked body. Since being initiated into nudity on the Greek islands I felt my body was akin to nature, with the same natural goodness. I loved my strength and agility and was proud of my physical strength and freedom. But my boldness was to trip me up.

We went out on group trips every few weeks and this one was to the Red Sea. Ten of us bumped along for an afternoon in the back of an open top lorry with narrow wooden seats along the sides and a flapping canvas overhead protecting us from the sun. Rosemary laughed loudly when she slid off the seat as the lorry made a sharp bend. We arrived in the evening and walked down to an empty beach. Straight ahead of us was a diving board leading out into the water. Everyone was talking and walking along slowly, but I suddenly felt claustrophobic and wanted to be out of the communal group.

I strode down to the water, stepped onto the diving board and walked to the end where I swiftly disrobed. I stood naked, certain all eyes were on me and took two sure steps towards the end of the board, bounced cleanly and dived in. I felt clear and powerful, flaunting my agile body. I swum fast in the clear, very salty water, marvelling at my buoyancy, and turning back I waded out, reaching up for my clothes on the board and got dressed quickly on the sand.

As I went back up the beach I was expecting some response, hopefully admiration, but the beach was empty as the group had moved on. Only Tobi was waiting and watching me. I walked up to him smiling, still feeling invincible and strong. His chocolate-brown eyes framed by his black curly hair and beard looked sad. He said three words that surprised me so much my bravado went out like a light.

'You scare me.'

I stared at him dumbfounded. I wanted people to be impressed, not frightened by me. There was neither praise or blame in Tobi's response but I felt deflated. I felt seen in an entirely new way and it dawned on me that my independent self-expression ran the risk of alienating me. As we walked in silence along the beach the bigger picture sank in. How different our realities were. Tobi knew the inside of a tank and how to operate guns. He knew how to kill but he hated war. I was like a child trying to win approval. The Israelis could be disarmingly honest and, in hindsight, Tobi's directness was a gift. Back on the kibbutz there were to be more reality checks.

The illusion that was reality in the beginning here has changed a lot. People don't seem to be perfect anymore. Joseph was thrown out after twisting Susan's arm – he was given half an hour to get out. You're equal if you do as you should – keep to the rules but they don't try to understand the human reasons behind actions that seem to them obviously wrong. Violence is wrong, but Joseph was created by the tension around him – in him. Seems to me. But people mostly here are beautiful. We just miss Joseph.

I thought the kibbutz was enlightened in ruling itself and making its own laws, but an exchange took place I felt was acted on too brutally. A kibbutznik punched a volunteer and told him to go. It shook my idealism, the dream of perfect community. But it also took with it some of my dreamy way of being. Although at the time I didn't like what happened, its effect put me more squarely on my own feet and I felt more separate and objective. That day after work I walked a mile away from the kibbutz to a stand of almond trees in full bloom. Their pink blur in the distance had been calling me. I stood alone, surrounded by the rolling land, moved by their scent and presence, settling into the satisfying feeling of being alone with myself. I needed more of this. My heart ached as I looked up into the perfect pink blossoms. Spring was coming and I was restless.

John knew the territory of the hippie trail better than anyone. He was a quiet man, often found sitting calmly on the edge of lively conversation, listening, taking things in. Perhaps the cultural similarities were pulling me; over the weeks I spent more time with him and Rosemary. We had a playful jokey interaction together and Anja, Lena and Axel often joined in. John had travelled to India and back and I listened with interest when he started talking about travelling East again. I'd been on the kibbutz for four months.

Strange evening. Dissatisfaction, wanting more. Tried to write a poem. Wanted to paint but couldn't. Shabbats are always unreal. This one was spent sitting on the steps of the cheder ochel waiting for a phone call from M and D. India's besadah. Tonight the wind suddenly came from the desert warm and strong – the chamsin. Strangely brought peace.

Although they were rarely worried, my parents liked to know my whereabouts. I had decided to go to India and I told them. They said they were ok – besadah – with me going. It was late February, the desert wind was blowing from the south and change was afoot. Axel was going back to Germany and Tom had decided to return to Wisconsin for the first time in many years of travelling. Rosemary also was returning to England.

Threw the I Ching. 'Stagnation to increase.' I realised what was happening here – stagnation. I've been trying to prolong something thats good – trying to squeeze everything out. Feel very positive about leaving.

Tobi had a copy of the I Ching, and with its help I realised I'd been hanging on. Once I decided to leave I felt no hurry as to when. The days moved by as I savoured my friendships and mentally prepared myself for the journey east. I had another phone call to make as I needed some money for my trip. The phone box was outside the cheder ochel and I walked there across the lawn from my room. I dialled the English operator. I asked them to call my bank in Hampstead in London and reverse the charges. I heard the bank manager pick up the phone and cheerfully agree to pay for the call from Israel. Then he came on the line and asked me how I was doing, how was Israel, and what could he do for me. I asked him to send me twenty pounds on an overdraft and he happily agreed.

I wasn't surprised. I took it as part of the manna that seemed to rain down on me. I assumed I would have what I needed. The money arrived a few days later and I was set to go.

7

On the road again

April 15

> *Yesterday we stayed on Acco beach in a fisherman's hut. He was a nice guy – came up to us on the beach and fed us with mint tea, nuts, chips, eggplant and hashish. There were two boys around, maybe his sons. We went back to his hut when it began to rain. Next morning he gave John and me some breakfast: eggs, chips and fresh fish the two boys had caught in the river while they were swimming.*

I had again found a travelling companion I could relax with. John was calm and practical and our friendship was uncomplicated – just what I needed for the journey ahead. We had no destination in mind, just east, maybe India. John was keen to take a less travelled route and I picked up on his excitement. Our first stop was to be Cyprus, and from there our route would take us northeast up through Turkey from the port of Mersin in the South. Once we arrived at the border with Iran we would be back on the beaten track of the Hippie Trail that traversed west to east across Turkey.

I wrote to Izzy before I left to tell her what I was doing.

She was ensconced in a cave in the mountains above Matala with an Italian boyfriend, happy to go no further. Our attachment to each other had lessened and we were on separate paths. The bond that emboldened us to take off from England, find our feet in Greece, and navigate our way to Cyprus had loosened. After her parents called her home, other travelling companions took her place and I had sallied forth without her.

The ferry to Cyprus left early in the morning so we hitched to Haifa the day before. We made our way to Acco beach nearby where we planned to sleep. It was a grey afternoon and the grey sandy beach stretched for miles, with a few drab industrial buildings just discernible in the distance. It was remote and empty, a contrast from the warm conviviality of the kibbutz. Yet I relished the change. The loss of home comforts – regular meals, dry room and warm bed – held no qualms for me. I looked at the wide expanse of sand with the wind blowing through the grasses, and felt refreshed by the new vista and the unknown road ahead.

The fisherman, with natural Palestinian hospitality, walked over to us on the sand and invited us to eat with him outside his hut next to a river mouth. After it started to rain he beckoned us into the tiny one-roomed abode. On the wall in front of me, amongst the pictures of footballers and fishing boats, were rows of bared creamy breasts and pale thighs stretched open. Some choice pages from porn magazines had been cut out and glued on the wall. I felt disturbed, yet his manner to me was quietly respectful, so an odd fit, as if I was a creature with a different body to those displayed above our heads. Despite the porn adorning his wall, he was the total opposite of the Greek men who assumed I was willing flesh every time.

He cooked for us and the boys that evening, made space for us on his floor to sleep, and prepared a meal in the morning. It was a tight squeeze, since the little hut was crammed with nets and fishing tackle as well as his own narrow bed. At the time I didn't take in the poverty and simplicity of this man's life out of which he gave so much. I identified myself as a traveller owning little and living simply, yet the truth of our realities was so different.

In the morning on the boat we met Tarben, a Danish volunteer from the kibbutz. Arriving in Cyprus, the three of us decided to spend a couple of days together visiting ancient sites, after which Tarben planned to go down through Syria to Babylon. He had managed to acquire two passports, one without an Israeli stamp, giving him the freedom to travel to Arab countries. John and I then set off to hitch up to the northern tip of Cyprus. On the last stretch we got a ride on a tractor, hanging off its sides as it chugged along. We were following the Karpas peninsula close to the coast and after several miles our friendly farmer stopped and turned around to us smiling, indicating he was turning off.

We clambered down through sand dunes to a long and

exquisite expanse of untouched beach. It was hot, still and empty. It was named, we discovered later, Golden Beach, known as the birthplace of Aphrodite. I took off my rucksack and stripped everything off with glee, stuffing my clothes into my bag and returning it to my shoulders. At last to be naked again! I had missed that freedom in Israel, the kibbutz being like a little town, always peopled and busy. I walked along enlivened, drinking in the cool air on my skin and the soft feel of my long hair on my back. My feet tingled with sensation with every step I took, pressing into the delicious texture of the warm sand, yet firm enough to make walking easy.

John followed suit quickly and caught up with me, naked as well, and we strode along. Ahead of us were several miles of virgin sand and in the far distance, perched on the promontory, was the monastery we were aiming for. We were told the monasteries offered free food and accommodation to travellers, and this one, on the final outpost of the island, we hoped would accommodate us. After exclaiming about the beach's beauty we walked along quietly. Out of the corner of my eye I saw something waving about in front of John's middle. His penis had risen like a pennant and was swinging from side to side as he walked. He was a step back from me, maybe hoping his body's response went unnoticed. I saw it but ignored it for I was in bliss. I wanted nothing more than the joy I felt in my body. And so we continued, with John a step behind me with an uplifted bowsprit whimsically pointed across the miles to the monastery.

A bird's eye would have seen two tiny figures slowly traversing the golden swathe, their bodies hardly distinguishable in colour beside a curving wash of turquoise sea. At times these little creatures ran headlong into the blue-green, agitating the smooth surface, their laughter drifting up, emerging onto the gold again, leaving concentric rings widening quietly out across the bay. Then moving slowly along again, until the bird could see nothing more than shadows at the end of the beach.

The sun was lowering as we came closer to the monastery and we donned our clothes then climbed up several stone steps to a hefty wooden door. It was opened to us by a serious monk in long black robes who stood on the step blinking in the last bright rays of sun. In response to our request for accommodation, he turned without a word, and led us along dark corridors to a gloomy kitchen where large pans were laid aside on an old cooking range. He spooned out rice and stew for us and we sat down to eat at a long table in a strange echoing dining room. The stew was cold and greasy, but we were hungry. We drank deeply from the tap, filling our glasses again and again. It was strangely quiet, but cool and dim, restful after the hours on the sun-swept beach. We saw no other monks and when we rose to wash up our plates, the same monk reappeared and led us to two separate cells to sleep. I lay awake on a narrow pallet bed in the silence, staring up at a small dark blue rectangle shot through with stars.

Forewarnings

The author in the Turkish mountains

April 20

> *On Cyprus we travelled around for four days sleeping in a monastery and beaches. Everything seemed to be given to us; food and lifts and places to sleep. It seemed like paradise compared to here. Now staying in a strange hotel in Mersin with Tarben and John.*

The next day we took the boat from Kyrenia across to Turkey. We booked into a hotel near the port and found Tarben ensconced there already and we shared a room.

There was a gallery running along outside our door overlooking a central courtyard. In the morning I heard the sound of water and looked down. A woman and two men were sitting silently next to a fountain. Even though it was sunny and the water splashing into the pool sparkled, there was a strange stillness that didn't feel friendly. They were staring into space, unmoving, and I couldn't understand what was going on. Everything felt more foreign here. We had breakfast in the hotel and when we spoke of our plans to locals in the bar, they warned us not to hitch across northern Turkey. Later in the town, others said the same, warning us in urgent tones bandits would rape me, take our money, and kill us. John ignored them. He had hitched to India before and assured me our route was fine. I believed him. We parted ways with Tarben who had decided to travel to Jordan.

We walked out to the edge of the town, stopping where the land began to rise, kicking our heels in the dust as we waited for a lift to take us north. The sun was hot, the road ahead through the mountains to Gaziantep wild and mountainous, and nothing was moving.

After an hour a gleaming mass of glitz and colour appeared on the empty road and screeched to a halt by our feet. A huge, swarthy, unsmiling truck driver gestured for us to get in. Like other trucks we had seen in the town, his was bright sparkly pop art on wheels, garish painted patterns with coloured lights and ornaments all over the bonnet. We climbed up high into the cab and sat next to the large sullen man.

We sat in the cab with him hardly speaking as we roared along remote forest roads and through tiny hamlets. As the light faded we drove up the side of a mountain until suddenly he swerved off the road and parked up next to a roadside building, lit dimly from within. He gestured for us to go in with him. We climbed down from the high cab and went inside a warm, smoky, primitive café. He led us straight through to the back where there was a badly lit kitchen. He was clearly a regular customer as the cook hailed him in greeting, grinned at us and lifted the lids from several steaming large vats of food for us all to look into. This was how it was done; customers were expected to go into the kitchen to inspect and choose their food. Our driver sat down with a group of men and engaged in lively talk while we sat at another table, quietly eating a hot spicy meze. A din of strange words surrounded us and I kept my eyes down as deep male voices resounded in vociferous debate. I ate hunched over, glad for the smoke-filtered light, and felt the rough chair scratching through my ever-thin skirt. But when he had eaten, our truck driver got up, gestured at our food and turned and paid for it. It was so unexpected. Such a surprise to have this dark, seemingly ungracious man pay for our meal on top of a long ride. I remember the graceful gesture of his arm rebuffing our thanks, then heard his lorry roar to life and accelerate off. We guessed he lived nearby and this was as far as he could take us.

It was pitch black when we emerged and we couldn't see in front of us, but we needed to sleep. Parked up along the side of the building was a big shadowy truck. We unrolled our bags and crawled underneath it and slept soundly on the concrete. I didn't think once that night it might be driven off! We woke to a cold day and went inside the café for something to eat. Then we started hitching. There was not much on the road, but we were heartened by our experience with the lorry driver.

After walking for some hours, a small car that had driven past earlier came back and skidded to a halt, its back tyres sending up a spray of stones we jumped back quickly to avoid. It was a little two-door hatchback with two men inside. We squeezed into the back and the car sped off. They seemed in an enormous hurry and spoke loudly and urgently to each other. John and I squashed together in the back, watched them uneasily. Suddenly, the man in the passenger seat turned round brandishing a thick wad of money. He waved it urgently at us, pointing at me and jabbing the money at John. I was sweating, intensely aware there were no back doors. I was wearing a cheap ring on my wedding ring finger as an attempt to deter the amorous advances offered to me in Mersin. But this was not amorous. The man wanted to trade.

We both pointed to my ring and told him firmly we were married. He carried on as if we'd said nothing, shoving the bank notes in John's face again while pointing at me, and again we said we were married and I held up my ring finger. He spoke in urgent tones to the driver then repeated his fanatical bargaining, banging the notes down on the back of his seat as he shouted. The emotional pitch in the car had heightened to breaking point. The driver careered along the mountain roads at a crazy pace and I was terrified. Nothing in my life had prepared me for this. The four of us were in intense close proximity in frenzied conflict while driving flat out along a bumpy mountainous road.

And I was being seen as a purchase that a dirty pile of banknotes could buy.

Then John began to breathe in a different way, slowly and evenly. I turned to look at him and he seemed to be concentrating all his will and energy into a single point. The man repeatedly barked his demand but when John next said, 'No,' it was different. His voice had dropped to a cold steely tone. There was a quiet force in it that was utterly resolute. For a moment it halted my own frenetic panic. Something had shifted in the atmosphere.

Very slightly, the man lessened his force, though still insisting angrily. John held his focus, staring fiercely into his eyes. Gradually the intensity of the demand weakened. The situation was still dangerous; we were in a very isolated area, but the mood was starting to turn.

The feverish bartering petered out to a moody silence and the car slowed and then braked sharply to standstill. Sullenly the younger man got out and we emerged on a dusty mountain road stretching out for miles. As the car accelerated away, my legs shook so violently I could hardly stand. Exhausted and shocked, we walked off the road along a path to the edge of a roughly cultivated field.

In the dusky light I knelt down, swept away a few stones and unrolled my bag a few inches from John. I climbed in, pulling the drawstring tight above my head, so all of me was inside. I curled up in foetus position, closing off the outside world, slowly repossessing my body from the numbing shock.

I woke at dawn to feel my sleeping bag strangely heavy. John groaned beside me in a muffled voice: 'Damn, I'm wet!'

I sat up to find myself enveloped by a counterpane of snow sparkling in all directions.

I screamed in amazed delight.

'Wow! We're buried in snow!'

The soft surprise of all that whiteness after months of browns and greens was refreshing. I loved it. Its unannounced arrival was like a deliverance from the day before and I welcomed its silent materialisation. I climbed out of my bag, shook the snow from it and gathered a pile of the freezing stuff in my cupped hands and washed my face.

Back on the road, our next lift was with a man who smiled and seemed friendly. John turned round from the front seat and we exchanged glances. Was it ok? We were spinning dice now with every lift. What would happen this time? I still couldn't sense the Turks. This guy spoke a lot, assuming we understood him. We drove for a couple of hours then he turned off in front of a garage – we assumed to refuel. But it was closed and after some moments of confused pidgin English and gesticulation, we understood it was his home and we could stay there. He took us round the back of the building to a door and opened it. I went through, but he barred John from entering with his arm. He shook his head and repeated something. Looking inside, I saw several women lift their heads to look, and realised this must be the women's quarters. I went back and told John who was outside the door trying to communicate.

I saw him being led off round the building and turned to find myself in a big warm room with coloured hangings and soft low couches with six or seven women talking quietly. The atmosphere was relaxed, but I was nervous not knowing where John was. An old woman in the corner watched me as a young child played next to her. I walked across the floor, which was soft and bouncy underfoot as if there were many layers of carpet. Two young women came over and greeted me in low tones. They were wearing traditional salwar, Turkish bloomers, with long tops in salmon pink and pale yellow hanging down over them. They sat me down on a sofa picking up strands of my hair to look at, murmuring in Turkish while they did so. They examined my hippie clothes and patched skirt, shaking their heads. I was offered a plate of soft little sugary balls tasting of almonds and roses. While I ate, they sat talking together quietly, throwing serious glances at me. The atmosphere was muted and felt strange, but I began to relax.

There were loud voices outside. I heard John and I stood up. The women whispered as I picked up my rucksack and opened the door. In the darkness two figures were standing, breathing hard as if they had been struggling. One stepped toward me. It was John and he grabbed my hand.

'In here, Carrie.'

He pulled me into a room lit by a bulb swinging from the ceiling half full of oil drums. He slammed the door and energetically started piling the cans against the door, explaining between breaths.

We have to . . . stop him . . . from coming in . . .'

He hauled the last can up to shoulder height onto the tower barring the door.

'John, what's going on?'

Under the harsh electric light he turned and looked at me, looking pale and tense.

'He has a gun.'

With a grim smile he returned to his oil can barricade, shaking it to check it was firm.

'Now he can't get in without waking us if we fall asleep.'

Harsh sounding words were shouted outside, and a bolt was shoved across. We looked at each other.

'Ok, he's locked us in. All we can do is wait.'

John sat down against the wall of oil cans. I sat facing him. I didn't feel frightened. The gun felt abstract and unreal. I felt dreamy, not unsafe, just dismayed to be stuck in the grungy petrol-smelling room. Interminable hours passed sitting under the bare light bulb, occasionally hearing the women's voices through the wall.

In the early hours a lorry screeched to a halt outside. I woke cold and stiff, slumped sideways on the floor. Through a tiny gap we saw a lorry driver climb down from his cab and walk towards our building, shouting for fuel. Suddenly, our door was unlocked and pulled open. The oil can tower wobbled, lurched, and crashed down through the doorway, missing the driver by inches. We jumped to our feet wide awake. I stood poised, ready to move fast.

The man jumped backwards, dazed, and we streaked out, leaping over the cans. I turned for a moment as we ran across the forecourt to see if anyone was following.

'Keep moving, Carrie, keep moving', John whispered urgently, striding ahead of me.

We were soon out on the road. John was staring and

pale, loping along. I was breathless, half running to keep up with his long legs. After some minutes we stopped and turned to look back. The road was empty.

'John it's ok, he's not following. We can slow down.'

We walked on at an easier pace with occasional backward glances. Both wired and jumpy. Neither wanting to risk another lift. Lorry drivers seemed safe, but nothing passed us. We walked on for a couple of hours until we came to a roadside café.

All eyes turned as we walked in. Trying our best to ignore them we sat at a table by a window. I slipped my sandals off and rested my feet on the cool floor.

'In the night – what happened?'

He inhaled deeply.

'After you went to the room with the women, he took me to the oil can room and started fiddling around with the gun, handed it to me after taking out the bullets, wanting me to admire it. I handed it back and he got me to follow him outside where he pushed me against a wall and pressed it into my stomach. Then he tried to bargain for you in bad French. I almost laughed, it was so ludicrous – and snowing as well. I managed to stand on a concrete plinth that gave me some height and pushed away his gun.'

I looked at him, unable to take in the danger we'd been in.

We sipped steaming lentil soup served with lemon slices and bread and began to revive. Then we walked again, covering the miles. My feet were sore but nothing else to do. We knew we wouldn't hitch again.

In the evening the lights of a town appeared. It was Erzurum and our steps lightened in relief. Our journey would be safe from here as this was on the main route east from Istanbul. We were right. As we entered the town we saw western travellers in the streets, the first we had seen since Cyprus. I was so glad to see them. It had taken us four days to hitch up through Turkey from Mersin, passing through Malatya and then a long flat road all the way to Erzurum. Doğubayazıt was up ahead and Bazargan was on the border. Our crossing point into Iran.

Carpet beaters by the river, somewhere in Iran

On the Hippie Trail again

April 25

Dazed and exhausted, we sat for hours in a small café off the main drag through Erzerum. I was in a stupor, hardly able to believe we'd made it. Long-haired travellers chatted and laughed around us. Talk of a journey in the Magic Bus from Istanbul drifted over from the next table and I began to feel a good measure of pride. We had come through a wild and dangerous route intact and one that few others ventured. A grubby little boarding house gave us a room, but I couldn't sleep, the adrenaline still charging through my system. The reality of the danger we'd been in caught up with me and waves of fear came and went all night. I was grateful for dawn. We boarded a local bus which would take us part of the way to Doğubeyazıt, thirty miles from the border.

When it stopped at Agri we got off and walked, nearly a hundred miles still to go. We were on a long high flat road cut between mountain ranges and I relaxed into an easy pace. My feet were beginning to harden from all the walking and I was happy to be on the well-travelled hippie trail.

In the hazy distance we made out a group of people standing round a bus by the side of the road. On reaching them we found a group of Dutch and American travellers making the best of a breakdown, sharing out food and water. We sat round a big fire with them that night, guitars reflecting the flames, and we sang away the vestiges of our traumatic trek. An English woman was keen to hear of our adventures and my voice trembled as I described the events of the last days. It was cathartic to tell and a relief to be heard. The firelight and shadows lent a dramatic backdrop, and in people's expressions round the fire I saw expressions of respect.

In the morning we left them tinkering with the bus. Within minutes a Ford van heading for Tehran stopped. Two French guys welcomed us aboard. It was great to be coasting along with two easy-going friendly people. Soon we were at Gürbulak, the border into Iran where we had a hassle-free ten minute wait. From there we swung through Bazargan and then took a route along the Caspian Sea. That night we slept on its cold and beautiful shore. Although this was a circuitous way to Tehran it was worthwhile to see this great body of water, a sea to some and huge lake to others. I walked along the water's edge in the morning enjoying the long emptiness of shoreline, grateful to be alone and feel safe. I imagined I could hear the voices of the Kaspi, the ancient people who lived there who gave the lake its name. I looked across the great stretch of water for the other side but could see only water. I'd heard it was landlocked so it must be a lake and I bent down, cupping my hand to lift a little water to my lips. It was slightly salty and I was confused and I returned to the van with questions to ask. But everyone was too hungry and impatient to answer why a freshwater lake was salty, and we drove off, stopping at the first shop we could find to buy bread and home-made yogurt.

The yogurt was sold in ceramic bowls and we sat eating in a dusty side street. The shop owner came out with a bowl in his hand and signalled to us to watch him. With undiluted pleasure, and an arm move to impress a cricket team, he swung it against a wall shattering it, adding to a big pile of broken shards. When we were done eating, the three men demolished theirs with glee, but I carefully cleaned mine, enjoying the colour of the warm brown glazing that was shiny inside and dull on the outside, reminding me of the bowls of yogurt from Mama's café in Matala. I put it in my rucksack where it survived intact for two days until falling into small pieces, proving its intended disposability.

Later we stopped by another café. We walked in single file through a dark narrow room to a bar at the back. The talking stopped as old men's eyes followed us, with only the bubbling sound of hookahs rising from the tables. We drank coffee in silence, then after twenty minutes men started to drift over to our table. Soon a crowd stood round us, curious and talkative. One or two spoke a little English and translated for the others. Afterwards we drove through the night with our French friends to Tehran, pulling up at a hippie hotel teeming with westerners.

Tehran

April 28

Staying in Amir Kabir hotel in Tehran for the second night. Saw so much today. There are patterns and flowers and colour in front of my eyes. Almost too much to take in. This morning I went with John to a museum. Such work in the weaving and stitching. So many hours. Now many years later each picture and cloth just sits quietly, at peace from the hands, breathing alone. The people hassle less here in this big town than in Athens, but they all seem different and hard.

Gone now are the chance of long walks solitary and meditative. See more and more how much joy and peace there was on the kibbutz. Every time I come into some situation where there is the security of people, food and a bed to sleep in – like the kibbutz, I feel nearer home, even though its been physically further away each time. Understand Izzy's song now. 'A hundred miles, a hundred miles, distances and time lie in our minds…'

My diary hints I was tiring of the unfamiliar. Even the embroidery was over-stimulating. I still needed time to digest the strange and scary days in Turkey but a stream of travellers circulating through the hotel gave me no space for myself.

John also wanted out of the busy capital and so we set out for Isfahan, a smaller city three hundred miles away.

We got a ride to Qom in a small truck loaded with baskets of dates and figs and it dropped us by the side of the muddy river Qom that runs through the city. We were told it was another sacred town that drew pilgrims. We walked peacefully through the town enjoying the light on the gold domes and ancient buildings until we picked up another lift to our destination.

Qom

Isfahan

May 6

We spent five days in Isfahan sleeping in Koudak Park. Then we went to see the shaking minarets and Atashgah the fire temple. Walked along the river through old Isfahan. There was a spring, a small round well, filled with the best stones I have seen. Mohammed appeared and asked us to have tea in his garden. We met his brother and many other students. They're like moths every time. Next day we came in the evening and slept inside the hut, and the day after we went with Mohammed to have tea with his mother, grandmother, sister-in-law and many sisters and brothers. Sitting on a rug under the cherry trees with pistachio nuts and tea, with staring and questions. Still, it was peaceful.

In Isfahan we found the Zayandeh River and walked through a great leafy classroom along its banks. Large trees offered wide green umbrellas of shade under which groups of men sat engrossed in animated or deeply serious discussion. Young studious men were everywhere. They were standing, talking quietly in groups or walking along, all holding books. None of them, unlike others on the streets, paid us any attention. Some walked slowly past us with heads down reading. Everyone was focussed on learning. The atmosphere was very different. We must have been close to the university, but the students weren't having fun. The place was charged with mental absorption.

Suddenly the spell broke as if cloaks of invisibility had been pulled away. We had been singled out. A young man made a beeline for us and fired questions as others glided up in curiosity. He introduced himself as Mohammed and told us the names of his brothers and their friends. They asked us where we were staying and when we said we hadn't decided, they beckoned to us towards a path leading away from the river. A few yards along it a little hut was hidden away, where we slept that night.

The next day Mohammed searched us out and invited us to tea. We followed him along the streets of old Isfahan and come to a door in an old wall. He opened it and we walked into a large walled garden heavy with the scent of cherry blossom. Sitting on large white rugs under the trees were his family. No men were present, just women and children. All eyes fixed on us as we approached. We were invited to sit down with them and were offered tea in glasses and little bowls of delicious nuts and sweets. We were stared at intently, but the curiosity was friendly.

Later we went to his house for more tea and supper of rice, chicken, beans, yogurt, onion leaves and radishes. Just a big clean room with carpets and cushions, a big fridge in one corner, and a place to hang clothes. Next door were two looms with two nearly finished carpets, being made by Mohammed's sisters. The smallest one about nine…

We were given an address to return to later and there we were treated to another wonderful spread together with Mohammed's mother, grandmother and little sisters.

The rice was bright yellow with saffron and the bowls of vegetables and meat steaming hot. The children were quiet and listened as Mohammed translated questions and answers between his mother and us.

'Do you have children?'

'No, no children.'

'My mother says why no children? You must have children, she says. See there.'

His mother pointed energetically at a doorway and we got up and looked into a room. Completely filling the space were two great vertical looms. I felt someone watching me and turned to see the youngest of Mohammed's sisters eyeing me intently. She was small and thin with expressionless small, dark eyes. I looked back at the looms.

By the nearest one, a shuttle wound with silk had been laid down on a wooden stool. I stared at the bright pattern winding round the rollers, colours twisting and repeating.

They were vast works, several feet square. I couldn't piece this huge and complex work together with the slight figure watching me, her two small hands passively hanging at the end of two thin arms. When I turned to try and say something to her about her work, her slight figure was moving swiftly out of the door into the sunlight.

Her mother shouted at her, demanding she return. Then with the same authoritative voice she called us both to the loom and gesturing to the two other girls, pointed at us to sit on a row with them on a narrow bench. The two older children laughed as they squeezed in between us and the thin dark-eyed girl slipped in next to me. Straight away the slim brown hands moved like quicksilver, pulling and pushing the threads and fabric, working the shuttle in and out. Then they stopped, and with much laughter, painstakingly showed us how to do it. The small girl, ever serious, handed me a shuttle and gestured where I should thread it.

I felt slow and clumsy in comparison, but with the children's help managed to weave a few stitches and I left the house feeling gratified. A fragment of our handiwork had been woven into the carpet in that house in Isfahan. I wondered where it might end up – perhaps somewhere in Europe, or even further East, the great carpet would bring colour, warmth and beauty to someone's dwelling. No one would ever know a couple of scruffy English travellers had contributed to its wholeness.

The Heron

The next day in the heat of the afternoon we visited the Shah Mosque. As we approached across the wide square, the huge porch glittered brightly. I stood and gazed upwards at hundreds of shimmering shining tiles. It seemed impossible that each one had been uniquely shaped, painted, fired and fitted in place. I pulled out a thin scarf I'd acquired for such instances, and tied it round my head as the mosques in Iran asked for more propriety than those in Cyprus. The cool interior hit me with a wave of pleasure, making it easier to take in all the detail. Everywhere we gazed shining colours shone back. The entrance portal was incredible, covered in tiles in seven colours: dark blue, light blue, white, black, yellow, green and beige. A wide inscription with religious text in Arabic was written in white, framing the inside of the Iwan, or hall. The guide told me the mosque was decorated with an extraordinary 475,000 tiles.

We wandered around. At the central point under the dome I whispered something to John and was amazed to hear my voice amplified all round the mosque. A clever architect had created this sounding spot just below the dome.

It was time to move on from the beautiful and prosperous city of Isfahan. We passed a group of laughing young women in jeans and bare heads looking relaxed and happy. We never imagined in a few years' time there would be a revolution that would change the country from a pro-western monarchy into an anti-western authoritarian theocracy. Innocent of future change John and I strolled out of the city. It was afternoon and we walked a few miles and took a path leading to a river. We arrived at a sheltered glade that looked like a good place to sleep. I walked through long grasses to the river. My brown sandaled feet came to a standstill in mud-stained grass just where the ground gave way to paludal marsh. Beyond a few tall reeds the water drifted slowly, uniformly brown, a reflection of fading blue light on its smooth surface.

In the middle of the river a heron was standing motionless on one leg. We were both still, the heron and I. It gazed downriver and I gazed at it. As I watched I was held by something more than stillness. In that moment the bird seemed greater than bird. This elegance rising from the water stopped my thoughts, arrested me from the long hot jostling day with its torrent of unintelligible words, and calmed my eye.

After the sumptuous feasting of blue on blue, the holy exquisite work, intricate mosaics arching against a brilliant sky, each tile way above my head a tiny blue wonder, here was peace. All that roar of blue beauty was faded in the river, calmed by brown with a pale blue reflection. And the heron, unmoving and unremarkably grey, held me in its animal presence with nothing else but itself. In doing so it pierced my memory more than any other single thing that day.

Back from the river was a little square concrete hut with a flat roof. We were laying our bags down beside it to sleep when we heard voices. Three nervous children appeared. The tallest boy stepped forward and spoke urgently.

'You must go. No good here. Bad men come from Domba with sticks. They will beat you. You must go quickly.'

I sat leaning against the hut looking at his long serious face, registering his words but feeling no impact. Everyone we met in Iran had been friendly. Unable to persuade us to go, the children left, calling back as they walked away: 'It will be bad for you if you stay'.

I sat looking at them leave and something inside me coalesced. I didn't want to go on. The landscape that had felt alluring and exciting in its foreignness suddenly looked alien. I thought of my friends at home, the place waiting for me at art school, and the whole familiar atmosphere of England. A total contrast to where I was now. The feeling that had been forming half consciously in the last few days became clear. I had an unfamiliar yearning for home. Perhaps the children's warning, or perhaps the heron had brought a sea change. The bird's still presence had lodged in my bones and I felt different.

'John, I want to turn back. I've gone as far East as I want to go.'

John didn't look at me. He was studying the gap in the two fields where the children had disappeared, and gave a small smile.

'I had an inkling you might turn round. I'm not sure I agree with your decision – that it's right, but it's yours to make.'

I knew he would be disappointed. I tried to explain:

'It's just got clear. From here I would be going all the way, there would be no half measures, no turning round. Once in Afghanistan, that would be it.'

With these words I had a strange mental flash. I saw myself in India. My hair was long and matted and I was thinner. My skin was dark brown. I was standing by a fire made in a hole in the ground looking into the flames and I felt heavy-hearted. This me had lived through more life and hardship than her nineteen years could manage. A spark had gone. My joy had dried up in the dust at my feet.

I felt jolted by the scene. I had seen myself having made another choice, as if a portal had opened in time and space.

Shocked by the intensity of the vision, I stammered:

'I . . . I have to return, John.'

John was still gazing into the distance. 'I'd like to write in your book'.

'What?'

'Your journal, I want to write in it before you go.'

I reached into my rucksack, touching my little 1973 diary, feeling past it for my brown note book bought on the kibbutz. John took it from me and wrote in the last bit of light, in his own made-up language and its translation. I lay on my back on the earth staring up into darkness, feeling a coolness on my skin. Returning was now or never, or anyway not for a very long time.

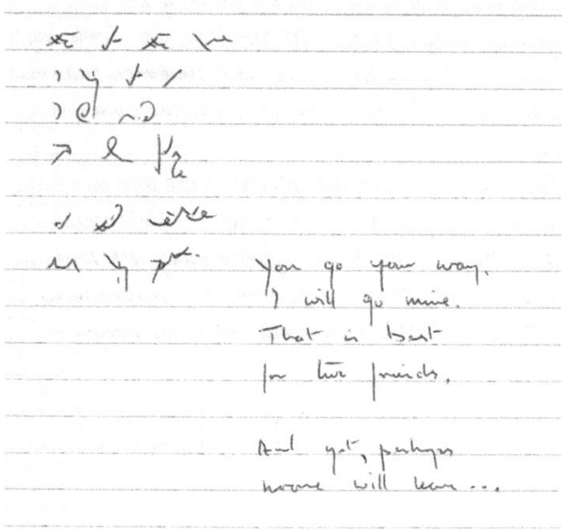

Next day we went to Isfahan and found a flute. Went to Atishgah and watched the sunset. I feel much stronger. The prospect of being alone tomorrow has cleared and brightened. Realise that imagination is the only frightening thing. Once those bad freaked out thoughts have gone and reality comes, I can be strong. Mohammed, his brother and a friend took us back on moped and bike. They worried about us sleeping there because of the bad people in Domba. 'I am worried for you,' Mohammed said earnestly. They wanted to watch over us while we slept! Mohammed always seemed to track us down in Isfahan. Despite their concern we still weren't worried and we waved them off and had a peaceful night.

After our second uneventful night by the river I woke refreshed, rolled up my sleeping bag and stood up with my rucksack on my back. John offered to walk with me to the main road where we had a simple leave-taking.

'Well, bye then.'

'Goodbye Carrie. Take care of yourself'

As I retraced my steps back to Isfahan I felt calm and clear, sure of my decision. I had seen the bus station on our explorations around the town and after an hour or so found my way there and the bus to Tehran.

Much later John told me what happened after I left. He had walked back along the dirt track behind a man with a donkey. He saw a huge pipe lying beside the track and had a strange impulse to climb up and balance along it and move in a kind of dance. He said it was like he was honing and balancing his energy for something. As he returned to his pack he'd left beside the hut, a clear inner voice told him to get up on the roof and lie down flat. He did so, lying on his back, flattening his rucksack beside him as best he could. Raising his head an inch or two he looked out between his feet. One small field away, four tall young men were striding purposely towards him. They had heavy staffs in their hands. A voice in his head said: 'Run'.

He scooped his bag up in his arms, jumped down, and ran, adrenaline fuelling his long legs in wide leaping strides through grasses and scrubby trees. He felt light and empowered, buoyed up in his flight, covering the ground like a gazelle, moving ahead of his fear. Directly in his path was a huge gunnera-type plant with giant leaves. He bent over, hardly slowing his pace, skidding in on his knees into a leafy den under its thick drooping greenery. Crouching there, quite still, he waited. Gradually, his pumping heart calmed. The next thing he knew was waking in the evening. He stood up and set off south-east towards Shiraz.

8

The Return

May 10

In the Amir Kabir hotel again I met Alice who is quiet and unassuming, travelling alone. She appeared just at the right time when I needed a little strength. I'm sure I won't see her again even if she ends up in England. She's someone I'd never meet there. It seems impossible to meet someone who's been thro so much, just in ordinary England.

I was on my own for the first time in the Middle East. In the bustling hotel my outgoing self foundered. I felt unable to approach the groups of people laughing and talking together, or to speak to other solo travellers. Feeling vulnerable I turned away from the café. I paid for a bed, then walked up some wide stairs to a long balcony leading to men and women's dormitories. I looked into a large room that seemed empty, then saw a woman sitting on a bed. She was doing nothing, looking quite content, and smiled as I walked in.

'Hi I'm Alice.'

'Oh hi, I'm Carrie.'

'I think all those beds are free', she said, gesturing to

the other beds.

'Thanks, I'm just here for the night.'

'Me too. Where are you headed?'

'West now, going home.'

'Have you been travelling long?'

'Eight months. Since last August. I'm ready to go back.'

'Yeah, I remember that feeling. But I'm pulled back east again.'

Alice had an unhurried place in her eyes. She put me at ease. We said little, but she spoke with tranquillity and her voice conveyed an inner security that gave me confidence.

In the morning after she left, I sat against the hotel wall witnessing the lively mix of townspeople and travellers coming and going. She had given me some thread and a needle, and I picked up a fold of my skirt and sewed a little piece of green sequinned cloth over a new tear. I had spied this fragment on the ground in Isfahan and picked it up knowing it would make a great patch. Sewing was the last thing I thought about on the scary journey through Turkey. I sat unnoticed on the hotel steps feeling happy, calmed by the rhythm of stitching.

Like all hippie hotels, information and choices about the next leg of the journey were easily found. With my confidence restored and ready to move on, I went to the hotel café to discover my options. I was offered hitching companions, a ride in a jeep, and someone tried to persuade me to turn back east, but I decided on the Magic Bus leaving for Istanbul later that day.

There was no definite destination time or even day. The two drivers said they would keep going till we got there, two or three days maybe. One would sleep at night while the other drove. No stress, no fuss, the usual hippie way, stopping for breaks night and day, chugging along. The bus turned up on time outside the hotel in the afternoon and hooted. I got in and sat next to a shy young man, more of a boy, who told me his parents were sitting behind us. He seemed glad to be heading back home to Germany. As we rolled through the night, the most comfortable position was leaning my head against the seat in front. I slept fitfully. I thought about my decision to return as the bus moved slowly west, and felt no regrets.

On the second evening I peered back at the empty floor along the length of the bus. Slipping down, I unrolled my sleeping bag, slid into it, and luxuriated in stretching my body out full length. I slept for several hours and when I woke, others had followed my example. The floor was a line of people lying head-to-foot down the corridor.

I arrived in Istanbul feeling refreshed. It was great to have discovered the floor space to lie down on. I got off the bus with the young man and his parents and headed for the Pudding Shop, the city's renowned hippie hub I'd heard so much about. Famished after the ride, I tried out the pudding the place was named after. I sat at a table outside and a surprising caramelised creamy chicken flavour hit my taste buds. It was delicious and I left the café energised, heading for the bazaar, my mind ahead of me, thinking of going home, wanting gifts for family and friends.

I saw a high ornate arch leading into the Grand Bazaar. I left the sunny street and entered a long corridor lined with colourful stalls. Sunlight fell in narrow shafts down from high windows. A strong smell of leather hit my nostrils, and tall piles of brightly folded cloth pulled my eye. Over my head numerous coloured glass lamps swung gently and I stopped to gaze at them. Instantly the stall owner engaged me in conversation, trying to lure me in. I didn't want the attention and turned away. I wandered on past a myriad of stalls packed with colour until there, just ahead of me, a tall slender man stood on the corner, talking animatedly to a stall holder, his hands gesticulating in wide curves through the air. I knew those hands.

'John! You're here? What are you doing here!?'

I was laughing. It seemed impossible. I had made a transition to travelling alone and I was bewildered to meet my travelling companion again.

'I got to Shiraz. Then I turned round', John said with a quiet smile. A typical understatement.

'So you didn't get to Afghanistan? Why? Did something happen?'

'No, it was fine, that is . . . until I got off the bus. I didn't want to travel east alone again. But I did something stupid when I got here. I left my camera on the bus.'

I was sorry to hear about the loss of his precious camera and empathised as we walked on through the market. I noticed a small picture framed in mother-of-pearl, and purchased it while fighting off offers of bigger ones. Back on the streets a sorry sight assailed us. A huge scarred and unkempt bear was standing up on his hind legs. A heavy rusty chain attached his foot to a lamppost. His handler was hitting him with a stick to make him roar, and a little boy was flitting through the watching crowd collecting money in a hat. It was a cruel sight. Despite his great height, the bear was a dishevelled, thin and miserable version of itself, and we moved on quickly.

John was upset about his camera. He still had a couple of rolls of unused film he'd carried from England in his rucksack. I told him he had given up too soon and insisted we walk to the bus station whereupon we were told to return the next day. We did, and to John's amazement, the station manager produced the dirty old sugar sack that he kept his camera disguised in, with his camera safely inside.

A day earlier, as Alice was leaving the Amir Kabir, she said I shouldn't leave Istanbul without visiting the women's bath. Later that day I stepped down a flight of wide marble steps through a doorway into clouds of

steam. In the dim light, great folds of dripping brown flesh confronted me. Although I was comfortable with nudity, this was different. The women were massive. As the steam cleared, I saw figures sitting and lying everywhere – on thick low marble tables, against the walls, or just standing in a dream. Everything was slowed down here, below the hectic street life above. All were silently in their inner worlds, gazing into the distance, prehistoric goddesses with enormous breasts, huge bellies, innately solid and powerful. A pervading sense that nothing could budge them, even if Istanbul took to flames above. Here was a ritual unchanged in centuries. Rooted and immoveable, the women were timeless too. I felt like a different being: too flighty, possessing too little. Although brown, I was pale in comparison, a mere insignificance to their wealth of weight and presence. I decided to ask for a massage but soon regretted it as an immensely muscled woman started to work on me, her huge hands encircling my waist, pummelling my shoulders and slapping my legs.

I walked away tingling and shaky, not sure about the experience. But my image of women had been altered. These proud earthy women, unafraid to fully inhabit their shape and their size, had left an imprint.

Reunited with his beloved camera John cheered up, and I was glad to be with my travelling companion again as my homecoming loomed closer. We found a Magic Bus destined for Amsterdam. The drivers seemed committed, as far as any hippie bus drivers could be. We were in the pudding shop having a last chai when John walked over to the notice board. He turned and looked at me with raised eyebrows as he pointed to a big notice slap bang in the middle of the board.

"Passenger wanted URGENTLY TODAY for London!
ASK IN P. SHOP."

'Wow!'

Without a word I went over to the counter to enquire.

This serendipitous offer was closer to my heart.

'Oh, that's William. His girlfriend decided to stay around here for a while so he wants a passenger. Not sure he can fit in two though . . . He just nipped out.'

We ordered more tea and waited. After some minutes a tall, willowy man strode in, had a few words with the waiter and headed over. He leaned on the table looking down at us in turn.

'Someone wants a lift?'

'We both do. We were going to take the bus but if you're going today we'll come with you. Have you room?'

'Guess so. Don't mind squeezing in, do you?'

Before the sun had set we were heading out in a camper van of unknown vintage and better days, roof rack piled high with boxes as the Grateful Dead sang out loud. William was English and had been to Afghanistan to buy Afghani wedding coats to sell in a London market. We gathered he had fallen out with his girlfriend who had come out from London with him. He said she was moving on.

Our first stop was a mangy café in Bulgaria. I'd been in the back squeezed between piles of coats stinking of goat and was relieved to get out. I was confused by the café owner shaking his head when I asked for tea. I wasn't expecting the reverse meaning for a nod now we were further west. In Greece, Iran and Turkey a nod meant no and a shake of the head meant yes, but despite being used to it, momentarily I forgot, and thought the café owner was refusing to serve us.

We carried on for some uneventful hours and stopped somewhere near Sofiya, as the mountain of Vitocha came into view.

By the side of the road William brewed up on the little stove in the van and we shared food we had bought with us. It was a cool night and I knew what would help.

'William, can we borrow a couple of your coats? Just to lay them over our bags. It's cold.'

'No way! I didn't go all the way to Afghanistan to get them filthy now.'

William became more and more taciturn. The next day we crossed the border with Yugoslavia and skirted up along the edge of the country heading for Belgrade, but it was no fun squeezed in the small space with him. Up a steep mountain side near Nis the van overheated and we stopped to let it cool down.

'Just what I needed', William said to no one in particular from the driver's seat. He sat dejected, his long arms folded haphazardly over the wheel. There was something giraffe-like about him, but without the grace. He seemed unable to manage the length of his lanky limbs. John and I got out to stretch our legs while he stared ahead moodily.

'Can we boil up some tea William?', I asked, hopefully.

'Nah, it's not worth it, we'll wait this out and go on. Won't take long.'

After the autonomy and freedom it was strange to be at the whim of someone's moods. We walked away from the van and sat on a rock looking at the view over the Nisava River.

After a while we heard the engine start and we hurried back. I wondered if we might find the van gone. William seemed quite capable of putting his foot on the gas and disappearing into the distance. But there he was waiting for us, not having left the driver's seat. As we carried on his gloom diffused through the small space of the van and I sank into lethargy, unable to avoid it. We rattled on through the countryside taking turns to sit in front, but neither seating option was that great. Either being pinned between piles of rank-smelling coats, or next to William.

That evening, desperate to get away, I walked across a field into a wood. I needed to be well out of sight and sound of anyone. The trees were big and silent and I stood with my back against a huge trunk trying to find some spaciousness in myself. I had had enough. On my return I told John I couldn't take any more. He was struggling too and I wondered why we had endured the joylessness for so long. The next morning we watched William drive away, grumbling to himself, and I flopped down on my back on the side of the road, stretched my arms out sideways and let out a long relieved sigh.

There were hundreds of miles to go, but free of William I felt lighter, happier with the journey itself rather than wishing my destination nearer. Despite our dour driver, our rides taking us towards Europe were a breeze compared to those in Turkey. After a couple of short trips with local farmers a black London cab stopped. Not a common sight on the hippie trail and I walked up in anticipation. I saw a woman in the front turn and the door open. I was full of expectation it was Sashi. But it wasn't her. It was Mary.

'Mary! What! How come? Where's Seb and Sashi? Isn't this their cab?

Mary gave a wide smile.

'It was their cab. I bought it from them dirt cheap. You may remember I crashed mine.' she said with a laugh. 'Something I won't forget. But now I'm in love with this gorgeous man.'

In the driver's seat a fair haired man turned and nodded, introducing himself as Vannis.

'Anyway, join us. Where're you heading?'

'England?!'

'Well we're going in your direction – to Belgrade.'

We got in and stretched out on the luxuriously roomy back seat. Mary turned and slid the intervening window open to talk.

'Vannis fixed this old thing up. He's a brilliant mechanic.'

Vannis spoke with an accent: 'Just needed some work but going like big bird now. Suspension caput. Sashi and Seb crazy drivers?'

I remembered with a smile the wild night journey down the rough mountainous track with Colin, Sashi and Seb.

'They did drive it hard. Off the road in Crete onto any old track. Once they took a steep way down a mountain, only just wide enough. Must have been a goat track. We had no idea where it would lead.'

'That's extreme, amazing the old thing still moves', Mary said, looking at Vannis who gave a long drawn out whistle.

'So, this why the suspension in pieces.'

Mary told us Seb and Sashi had left Crete to live on another Greek island, leaving the taxi behind. Time and miles sped by as we talked. As the outskirts of Belgrade appeared we asked to be let out as hitching would be better outside the town. I got out wishing I could go on talking with Mary. She was less extrovert and more present, as if her exploits on Crete had tempered something inside her.

But back on the roadside again I felt carefree. It was enlivening not knowing who would stop next. Before long a big black car came gently to a halt by our feet. A man with dark sunglasses leaned out, accompanied by a whiff of aftershave.

'Where are you going?'

I felt playful after our friendly journey with Mary and Pete and gaily replied.

'How about London?'

He laughed and replied he could take us across Austria into Germany. John got in front and I sank into a soft leather seat behind him, taking in the black upholstery and gleaming handles, and relaxed.

Our driver's name was Viktor and he was returning home from a business trip. John spoke to him and I looked at the back of his head, fascinated at the neat black hairline curving round his white neck. It was a rare sight. I hadn't seen such short hair in a long time. After a couple of hours he asked if we wanted to come back to his house in Munich for the night. John turned round and I nodded, feeling safe. The smooth ride lulled me and I dropped off, sleeping soundly all the rest of the way through Yugoslavia, across Austria and into Germany. I woke up sleepy and disorientated as streetlights flashed by the windows. We parked beside a large town house and got out and walked up some wide steps into a dark hall. A voice called out in greeting and a woman opened the door, flooding the hall with light. On seeing us, her smile froze. She turned on Victor with a torrent of German.

'Viktor, Du hast's schon wieder gemacht. Ich hab' Dich schon erzählt, es reicht mir. Wie oft muss ich denn wirklich Dich sagen, diese Trampern niemals wieder zuhause zurückbringen.'

(You've done it again Victor! I told you I have had enough. How many times do I have to tell you not to bring these hitch-hikers home?)

A harsh jumble of words tore across the room. They were meaningless to me but the emotion was clear. She was extremely angry. John nudged me and said quietly: 'We should leave.'

Victor, hearing him, said quickly: 'No, wait.'

And he steered his wife by the arm back to the kitchen.

We heard their raised voices gradually lower in tone, then Victor emerged beaming at us from the bright kitchen and told us his wife would show us where to sleep. Red-faced and angry, she led the way, muttering under her breath.

'Meine Güte!'

She opened the bathroom door, turning to us with fierce emphasis.

'Here is the bath, and here are towels.'

I realised we had acquired a strong goaty smell from William's vanful of coats, and I came to suddenly, remembering my manners.

'Oh thank you very much. A bath would be great.'

With head down she walked away moodily mumbling in German: 'Ich halte es nicht mehr aus . . .'

(I can't stand it any more)

I had no idea what she was saying. The angry words were a thunderstorm moving past some way off and her anger didn't penetrate. Towel in hand I locked the door and stood in the rare seclusion of a bathroom. I turned on the tap marvelling at the gleaming bathtub filling with steaming water. This was going to be a treat. The first bath in eight months. I lowered one begrimed foot into the fragrant silky water and sighed. The rest of me followed, and I lay looking down on my brown-skinned body and dirt-ingrained feet, soaking in the warmth. Under the white light my skin looked dark brown. When I emerged and dried off I stared at the black rim round the bath. I felt strange. Although refreshed and warm I felt a loss. Something of my travelling skin had been shed.

We drank coffee with Viktor and talked till late. His eyes were bright and hungry listening to our tales. He was clearly longing for the same kind of freedom. He would have talked all night but in the early hours his wife started knocking on the floor above us, shouting in a muffled voice. Victor showed us to a room and I lay in a soft bed uneasy and restless, unable to sleep. Finally I worked out what was wrong. I slid onto the floor and eased myself into my sleeping bag. Relieved to feel the familiar firmness, I fell fast asleep.

The next day it was drizzling. Our generous host took us to the slip road of an autobahn heading for Holland

and his hand waved goodbye out of the window as he drove away. But the sky was heavy and I was tired. I didn't want to be there by the edge of the road hitching. The cars were too fast, the noise was draining and the persistent damp was seeping into my clothes.

Another hitcher was standing on the verge ahead of us. He was crouched down searching in the grass for something. I walked over and suddenly he rose to his feet with a loud 'Yah!' As I got closer he held out his hand to show me a perfect four-leaf clover. He was a tall rakish German man and told me he had been looking for ages. I looked at the delicate green leaf with four perfect petals in his palm. I had never seen one before, and in the midst of the dreary, noisy place it was a miracle. He looked at me for a second then slid a thin book out of his pocket and carefully pressed the clover between two pages. Then he turned to face the road with his thumb out and seconds later a car had enveloped him, speeding away along the autobahn. When we finally got a lift I had no such treasure, despite a long and careful search through the wet grass.

Amsterdam

After all the timelessness
How can I tell of things timed?

Nearing home again, pausing here
The sun and everybody stepping in and out
Feeling the richness of past smiles and waters.

I wrote this sitting in a café on a busy street in Amsterdam. After a couple of nights in the "The Sleep Inn", a cheap and basic warehouse for travellers, we met an Indonesian woman who gave us jobs in her café as we were both broke. I was washing up and John preparing food, and we moved into a small one-roomed flat above. It was mid-May and it felt good to stop for a while there so close to England while I inwardly prepared for my return. I felt no rush to cross the channel. A maturity had grown in my travelling self, as if some part of my character had come to fruition. I felt I could sit back and observe life.

In our breaks we adjusted to European culture and pottered along city streets bubbling with life. Street sellers sold chips with spicy peanut butter sauce, and in the narrow streets of the infamous red light district we were gaily propositioned.

One day in our wanderings we chanced upon a large colourful building. Through an open door I saw a hallway in glowing tones of orange, yellow and gold. A wave of sweet pungent incense reached our nostrils as we walked in. A monk with a shaven head appeared and greeted us. I was fed up with washing up and sleeping in the dingy little attic and asked if we could stay. The smooth-faced monk looked at me and then at John intently, weighing us up.

'This is a place of worship. To live with us means joining with how we live. We are followers of Krishna. We chant and pray and work each day. You are welcome to follow our routine with us.'

We agreed to this arrangement. In return for attending the daily schedule and work we would have food and a place to sleep. I was drawn to living in a concentrated bubble of Eastern spirituality. There were thirty people living and practising the Hari Krishna faith in this little community. We peeped into the meditation hall, a large room covered in carpets with a huge ornate altar where a stature of Krishna and his sacred consort Radha perched triumphantly. The next day we left the café in the evening and arrived at the now dark, quiet building. A drowsy monk showed us to separate rooms, the strictly divided men's and women's sleeping quarters.

At 4.00am a bell rang and I struggled to open my eyes under a bare electric lightbulb. I wasn't expecting to rise so early. In the empty room filled only with mattresses on the floor women were standing up getting dressed. Slowly I sat up, seeing them showering in cold water in a shower cubicle in the corner. They dressed swiftly, winding sari-like robes around themselves. Here was none of the usual touchy-feeling hippie warmth, yet no one was unfriendly, just silently one-pointed, focussed on the basic actions needed for washing and dressing.

Declining the cold water I was last down, and descending the stairs a humming rhythm rose to meet me. Drawn through the archway into the meditation hall, I was enfolded in soft, warm candlelight, inhaling an exotic fug of incense. It was a relief not to be asked to talk or do anything and I settled down on the floor with my back against a wall. Seconds later I was asked to move forward by a shaven-headed woman in long orange robes. I could have used some support for my back so early in the morning, but as I joined in, finding my way with the words of the first chant, I grew more alert. This chant was the mainstay of the ashram.

Hari Krishna, Hari Krishna,

Krishna Krishna, Hari Hari.

Hari Rama, Hari Rama,

Rama Rama, Hari Hari.

Despite the early rise, this place of prayer was home to my soul. Chanting the holy names of God made me happy and energised. I had loved it from the start when Pierre first taught us the Sanskrit words and tune of a chant on the ferry that we had sung long into the night. Gazing at the altar aflame with light, I returned to the undulating dark water of that journey, and the joy I felt chanting as I stood on the bow of the boat after we had turned back from the war in Israel. I had felt so ecstatic I could have stood there forever.

Now, surrounded by the smoke of numerous incense bowls I again felt the unifying effect of a group singing together.

Afterwards I sat down with a dazed and sleepy John.

'Not sure about this', he mumbled, as he picked at a bowl of kitcheree, a mixture of spicy rice and lentils.

A nearby monk put her finger over her lips warning us that breakfast was in silence. I ate quietly and looked round at people and noticed they were all westerners. Hippies, I guessed, who had settled for a devotional path here in a western city after travelling east. We were put in charge of painting the spindles of the wide curving staircase. Sanding and undercoating was fiddly but we slowly worked our way up. It was quiet in the building and at lunch the place was almost abandoned.

'It's strange here isn't it?', I said, breaking the silence.

'Yes, and some way to wake up – in the men's room there's a bucket to pour freezing water over you while you stand in a big bath. They all shout, "I am not my body!". Madness – but it seemed to help.'

'The women said it too, though we do have a shower. But I love the chanting.'

We were told the monks had gone out into the city to walk and chant the Hare Krishna mantra and to sell the Bhagavad Gita. Spreading Krishna consciousness and street preaching was a visible public activity of the movement. The next day we were invited to join the expedition in the streets and I walked along, hardly able to chant, self-conscious and uncomfortable being seen in public with the orange-robed disciples.

After five days we decide to leave. I walked into the street feeling fresh and clarified as if all my cells had been scrubbed clean. I had never experienced such a feeling before. Although the food was pure and simple, it was in the many hours of chanting holy names that I felt as if I was being cleansed and refined. Life there had a simple clarity – just working, chanting and praying. Once I adjusted to the early hours I liked it, for those few days. Before we left we were given copies of the "Bhagavad Gita", the Hari Krishna "bible". The translation of the ancient Sanskrit scripture was printed on cheap paper with bright splashes of colour. I carried it in my rucksack as we walked through Amsterdam on our last morning there, heading for the main exit to hitch the last lap to England.

9

Home

May 27

My first memory of being back home in England is sitting at the gleaming dark oak dining table. The one layered with French polish that must never have anything hot or wet placed on it. I had not sat at this table for nine months and now my body was feral and estranged as if my shape had changed and no longer fitted. I looked down at the precisely arranged cutlery. It looked cold and remote in comparison to how I felt eating with my hands, a warm and gentle caress with the food.

The over-bright voices clattered across me as I stared down at my long silver fork. The smaller fork lay stiffly parallel, not quite touching, both engraved with my grandfather's crest gleaming on their shafts. To the right lay their partners that my right hand any minute had to engage with: the big bone-handled knife and later the silver dessert spoon. A little further away, the contents of my crystal glass glinted in the sunshine from the window. All of it seemed impossibly unwieldy. The meal was in celebration of my return. But round the table with my parents and brothers I felt paralysed, struggling to manoeuvre the cumbersome silver cutlery, to get it all right and behave as expected. However did I do it before?

I'm home. It was oh, so familiar, yet I was not. I was no longer someone who could sit at that table anymore, yet there I sat, forcing my wild nature body into place.

'So Carrie, how is it to be home again after all your travels?'

'I don't know really'. I mumbled, 'it's a bit of an adjustment to be back.'

My mother looked at me expectantly. She wanted more. An eloquent discourse on my trip. But I felt disjointed and displaced. Even though I had written long, inspired and coherent descriptions of places and experiences in my letters, now in the family home my sense of self was dissolving.

In my room I stared out to sea remembering a day when my trip was yet a dream. The sea still stretched towards the sky. The walls around me strong and still. The circle was complete. Was that it then? I'm back where I started? But no, on my bed I saw my skirt peeping out of my rucksack and I pulled it out. As I held it to the light, it was alive. The mirrors sewed on in Israel glimmered and flashed. All the colourful patches and darns reflected the me who had walked unafraid, breathing all the many different airs, and, the me who could face coming home, the hardest challenge of all.

I scanned its length, really seeing it here – in my childhood home. It sang to me of all the places I'd been, the thorns that tore its worn threads, the places I sat and sewed, all the people who gave me pieces of cloth to use. Crumpled in crowded buses, blown about in hot Meltemi winds, clutched to me as I clambered into Greek ferries, twisted up behind me on a battered old motorbike, dropping in still folds on a hot Turkish mountain. It lay ruffled round my crossed legs sitting silently in a mosque, and folded tight round me on cold nights in my sleeping bag. It walked with me along the many byways my journey had taken through Isfahan, Istanbul and Amsterdam. Now it's home, stained, worn and threadbare, telling me I'm not back where I started – and I smile, thinking of all I have done, felt and been. I feel *me* under my belt now, not only my parents' deep influence. The circle can lift now to spiral into life, for my heart had grown and my mind widened.

However hard this homecoming, nothing could take away what I felt and found with the help of my trusty friend Izzy who started out along the road with me, shedding her restraining clothes, to fly away like birds.

I laughed out loud remembering her determined face as she thrust her fuddy-duddy clothes out of the train window. I see them clearly, flapping wildly in the wind, and disappearing, as we adventured away together along the joyful road.

Afterword

After over forty years of no contact I decided to look for John, my travelling companion. All I knew was his name and that his father had been a doctor in Canterbury. I started by calling the health centres and hospitals in the city. After seven calls a friendly receptionist suggested I write an ad in the Kentish Gazette. Four doors down the road from John's house in Canterbury, where he had lived for forty years, an elderly neighbour read every single column . . .

That Spring I set off in my campervan from Devon. I wasn't well and drove only an hour or so a day. It took me a deliciously slow eleven days to get to his door. When he opened it his first words were: 'Come and see what I've got under the microscope – a very unusual spider . . .'

John's version

'Is this you?' she said, handing me a tiny scrap of newsprint. My neighbour had chanced upon this fragment while idling over a cup of tea; I should never have come across it myself for I rarely read the personal columns in the local paper. My name was missing an 'f' and the year of birth stripped me of a few years but the rest of it was correct: this really was from Carrie. How strange to be contacted by someone last seen over forty years ago; to be reconnected with memories that now dangle by a tiny thread. I kept no diary of our travels together for the past is past and that which is important does not need to cling to paper to be remembered. But memory proves fickle: some things I remember quite clearly she has no memory of and sometimes events that took place in the order I recall, her diary proves otherwise.

It is important to pick one's travelling companion carefully. In the past I had once hitch-hiked through Europe with someone not used to sleeping rough or to the vagaries of eating on the move. In time I grew irritated when I found I was doing all the work while he sat on the roadside doing little but complain. I learnt my lesson: choosing a fellow traveller has to done with care. They should be someone you are able to pass the day with without getting bored; someone who knows when to talk and when to be silent. They need to be someone you can rely on and trust to remain calm when the unexpected happens. I was lucky for I found these qualities in Carrie.

I do not remember how it was that she and I decided to travel east – perhaps at the time it just felt right. In those unshackled days our actions were often decided by a feeling, or by the fall of three coins as we consulted the I Ching. In the early 70s travelling through Turkey and Persia with a girl with fair hair aroused considerable interest. To this day I'm not sure if she was aware that I was often taken aside to discuss "arrangements" with a lorry driver, of if she realised that we were in a situation that could turn unpleasant. However there is a stillness that surrounds her, an air of calmness and serenity that perhaps prevented a situation from turning ugly. It gave me confidence; I could sense that nothing bad was going to happen to us.

We parted in Isfahan and while Carrie went back westward I spent a few more days living there until an unpleasant encounter with some local thugs forced me to move on and I left for Shiraz. Travelling with a friend is quite different than travelling alone and soon I felt the pull of India was not as strong as it had been. I now felt my journey was westward too and no longer towards the east.

We met again in the jingle-jangle of the Grand Bazaar in Istanbul and it was there I told her I had left my camera and a few other things wrapped up in an old sugar sack on the bus. I never thought I'd see them again but she thought otherwise and together we went to the bus station to report the loss. Next morning we returned and though still doubtful of success I was handed back my scruffy old sack by a smiling official. Sometimes the less experienced traveller has a better handle on life than the more experienced one.

Slowly I let the comfortable chains that bind one to a

place hold me down, and with that the freedom of youth was left behind; I no longer wanted to travel; I was content to stay here. For a while across this broad tapestry of life two people had together woven a picture, and then for years their threads had parted to fashion their own stories; and now slim chance had gathered then again and brought about full circle.

'Is this you?' she said clutching in her hand the tiny key to a world long ago . . .

In the dreamtime

It had been a hot day, perhaps I really had dozed off - but it could not have been more than mere seconds. She had been there sitting beside me as she is now; the same crystal clear eyes, the same stillness. Her voice, unchanged; but in those few hazy moments something was different. Across the water the bird flew over the lake its wings barely skimming the surface: the silence of distance. In the dreamtime perhaps forty years really had passed but how could it have. And yet, a tiny line across her forehead betrayed her. The circle had closed, touched, and all was still. Far off, a warbler sang its closing song of the day.

John Sefton. 10 March 2018

Glossary

A selection of words and phrases that were the hippie vernacular of the time, or at least mine and Izzy's.

Afghan: strong dope

Crash: to sleep

Crashed out: to be exhausted

Crack/cracked up: collapse in emotion

Flip out/Flipping out: stunned or amazed by beauty

Freaking out: frightened

Hassles: bother

Paranoid: terrified

Scene: love affair

Score: to buy cannabis

Split: to leave / left

Shattered: tired

Not on: untrustworthy

Together: clear-minded, organised, practical

Untogether: disorganised, all over the place

What!: amazing

Acknowledgements

The gift of having a small weekly writing group kept me on course to follow the long road out and home again. It gave me the time to develop my craft of words and that's no small thing. Thanks to you all: Michael Elsmere, River King, Clare Pawley, Christine Yates and Jean Mooney for your encouragement and just analysis. The group's initiator, Michael Elsmere, helped me believe in my book with his particular gift of explaining why, when it did, my writing worked.

I had a wonderfully sensitive editor. Wendy Watkins walked with me on my journey keeping me awake with her perceptiveness. Her awareness of inner processes along with a careful attention to detail were a godsend.

My four 'readers' each read these sixty thousand words in one go, leading me out of the strange isolation of wondering through a word-maze that took four years to complete. Thank you to Michael Elsmere, Ann David, River King and Fiona Green for following the lines to the end and picking me up on my faux pas. Ann David lifted my spirits with her addition of occasional little hearts in the margins!

The careful eyes of my proofreaders Peter Binns and Hafiz Ladell righted my dyslexic blunders. Much gratitude for your time and friendly observances. Jane Rogers and Edwyna Beaumont both read sections and gave me encouragement, and I greatly appreciate Sue Chapman and Ann David for lending me their houses for writing retreats away from all distractions.

I thank Hafiz again for the formatting: for kneading and shaping text and image via numerous emails that swished back and forth between us till all was cooked and ready.

John Sefton took me to the gardens of quiet pubs on the outskirts of Canterbury to mull with me over our various fragments of memory. I'm very glad we met again

I thank Jack for his letters and love as he travelled further east than I. His long missives waited in poste restantes on thin, pale-blue aerograms, reciting escapades from even less beaten tracks than mine.

Thanks also to everyone who told me they wanted to read this, my first book. The list of your names hung over my computer cheering me on. My brother Conrad affirmed its emergence by paying for a copy before it was printed!

My deep appreciation goes to my husband River King, whose keen critical eye noticed what others missed and whose steadfast love helped me relax and continue.

I have recreated my journey in these pages to the best of my integrity and remembering. All names have been changed to protect people's privacy. Conversations from so long ago cannot be recorded verbatim, but my spoken exchanges with people impacted me in powerful and formative ways and it is the essence and feeling of these encounters that I retell.

Caroline Born

I like dancing on the beach at dusk.

I am a movement teacher, a performer and an artist.

For 35 years I have facilitated groups in body awareness and movement, taking my work into prisons, hospitals, schools and universities.

I'm happiest when feeling alive and present in my body in both movement or stillness.

I live in a wooden house in Devon with my husband River, surrounded by sunshine, birds and strong winds.